A *Second* Look at White Ironstone

Jean Wetherbee

Cover Photograph: Perry L. Struse, Jr.
Boote 1851 Octagon Pieces Courtesy of Author

Cover and Book Design: Ann Eastburn

Library of Congress Catalog
Card Number 85-051342

ISBN 0-87069-444-8

10 9 8 7 6 5 4 3 2 1

Published by

Wallace-Homestead Book Company
580 Waters Edge
Lombard, Illinois 60148

One of the *ABC PUBLISHING* abc *Companies*

Contents

Acknowledgments

Compiling the information for this book would have been impossible without the help and encouragement of the groups and individuals listed here.

My friends and neighbors who lent me their pieces to copy for my first handbook.

The collectors who eagerly brought me questions, shared their knowledge, and showed me their treasured pieces: John and Beverly Black, James and Doris Walker, Carol and Gary Grove, John and Jane Yunginger, Mr. and Mrs. William Horner, Kenneth and Alice Johnson, Jane and Wes Diemer, John and Lois Rhines, Shirley Montgomery, Charles and Harriet Hoover, Sarah Province, Mr. and Mrs. Thomas Richardson, Mrs. Dawson Farber, Jean Hogg, Florence Travis, the Zerns, Dick and Adele Armbruster, Howard and Dorothy Noble, Willis Barsheid, Judy Young, Ray and Priscilla Casavant, John and Shirley Anderson, Margie Watson, James and Michelle Sempere, Eileen and Lionel Sirois, Sally and Howard Erdman, Carl Groetzinger, and the collection of the Museum of Texas Handmade Furniture, New Braunfels, Texas.

My daughter Linda who willingly and enthusiastically scouted, carried, and encouraged me to finish this task.

The readers of *A Look At White Ironstone* who wrote appreciatively, offered suggestions, enclosed sketches and snapshots, and kept urging me to compile another "look" book.

The editor of *Antique Trader Price Guide* who gave permission to reuse photographs included in that publication.

The individuals who lent pictures and the photographers who labored so long to "catch" the patterns in the excellent black-and-white photographs for this book: Lebel Studios, John Black, Harvey Phillips, Francis Bridges, Winfield Wetherbee, Susan Dollard, Adele Armbruster, Wes Diemer, and Paul Groff. And especially photographer Clarke Blair, whose creativity and advice improved this book.

Jean Ann Lyons who typed the text patiently and accurately.

And, of course, Wallace-Homestead Book Company and its editors who have made it possible for this white ironstone record to take form. Thank you all.

1 Considering White Ironstone

The feeling of early American rural life is recaptured in a row of large octagonal ironstone plates across a hutch, in the smooth lines of a white pitcher filled with black-eyed Susans, or in a giant soup tureen overflowing with zinnias. This white stone china is at home near a roaring fire on the grate, mellow pumpkin pine furniture, an old polished churn, and braided rugs.

White ironstone *needs* to be used. Men and women, old and young, now collect pieces to use as everyday dishes or for entertaining with flair. Some collect only one pattern, others group related motifs. A few search for the unusual, another may choose only sugar bowls, pitchers, or toddy cups. The typical fan buys what appeals to him and then narrows his field as the stoneware crowds him out of the house. With well over two hundred fifty patterns from which to choose, white ironstone keeps its collectors active.

The graceful lines of nineteenth-century white ironstone often are featured on the pages of country decorating magazines, where homemakers see the startling simple accent of white.

Always eager to learn more about these hardy nineteenth-century dishes, collectors have joined me in looking into the past. The following pages reflect what we've learned about white ironstone.

To find the "roots" of ironstone, we searched the English history of ceramics. *Ceramics* can be defined as all ware made of clay or fusible stone. When the English became fond of tea, they decided it tasted better when sipped from cups made of china rather than metal or rough earthenware. This made *porcelain* tea bowls or cups imported from China both desirable and expensive.

By 1550, the finest wares were imported into the British Isles from Germany. Like Germany, other European potters were trying to perfect a hard porcelain like the oriental wares. Near London, the English began to produce *delft,* an earthenware covered with a tin glaze. Its manufacture spread to Bristol, Liverpool, and other pottery centers. These wares, with a clear white finish that chipped easily, were a rather poor attempt at copying the whiteness and decorations of the fine oriental pieces.

By 1700, England was making stoneware that rivaled that of the Germans. It was made of special clays, then mixed with sand and fired at such a high temperature that it became partly vitrified, or waterproof.

A great period of creativity began in the Staffordshire area with the work of the Elers brothers, who made fine redware. They glazed their earthenware by casting salt into hot kilns, creating an "orange peel" appearance on the surface. Eight of their fellow potters were enraged at the resulting clouds of smoke that blanketed their potbanks.

Slipware decoration was made by trailing slip over the outside of clay bodies. This practice dated back to medieval times.

The Elers brothers introduced many improvements and, so the story goes, worked under great secrecy, only employing workmen who appeared to be dull-witted. Two young men, John Astbury and Josiah Twyferd, worked "under cover" in the pottery for two years, trying to learn the Elers's skills and methods.

In 1720, still trying to imitate Chinese porcelain, John Astbury produced a hard, strong, white body by adding calcined flint to light-colored clay. He, too, used a *salt* glaze, plunging the pottery settlement into partial darkness in the resulting smoke.

A new method of forming dishes was mastered as potters introduced molds, usually made of two or more pieces that were notched together and were easily removed after the clay body dried.

The early English porcelains, copied from the oriental or European decorations, were usually made from soft paste. A few firms made hard paste.

The discovery in Cornwall of clay earth gave more impetus to the china industry. At about the same time, some potteries were making fine, thin, white translucent wares, and were constantly improving the detailed decorations. The mid-century invention of transfer printing made potting even more complicated. The Staffordshire settlements during that century had a hard time competing, since their ware was often crude, opaque, and thick.

Josiah Wedgwood, a leader of the Staffordshire potters, made his acceptable cream-colored earthenware called *Queen's Ware* and, a little later, his *Pearl White*. They were both inexpensive forerunners of white granite, which was to be the main product of the other Staffordshire potters throughout the nineteenth century.

Meanwhile, the Chinese imports had become cheaper, readily available to the middle-class Englishman, and were imported in vast numbers.

All the experiments directed at improving porcelain also educated the potters who were to discover the ironstone bodies. The shapes of late eighteenth-century dishes that were to be carried over into ironstone molds included handleless cups (tea bowls), octagon shapes, leaf-shaped servers, sugar boxes, jugs, and coffee cans (mugs). They were all originally made in porcelain.

By the nineteenth century, the English pottery industry had split into two different groups. Pottery groups such as Minton, Copeland, Spode, Coalport, Worcester, Derby, Wedgwood, Doulton, and the Rockingham makers were engrossed in detailing ornate porcelains and bone china. It is the decorative wares of these firms that British ceramics historians proudly discuss. Meanwhile, the Staffordshire potters included in this book were mass producing wares that were useful first and decorative second. They aimed for the American market, where anything showy and rich looked out of place. In England, this durable, simple stone china was only good enough for the servant class.

The nineteenth century has been called the age of imitations and fads. Nevertheless, more improvements were made and more ceramics ideas were patented in the first half of that century than ever before. During this time, the Staffordshire potteries were competitive with each other, and were always alert to the protection of their large colonial market.

The Victorian Age in England ushered in a period of ornate decorations in architecture, home furnishings, and china. We have only to study pictures from this era to see the incredible skill and versatility of the ceramics masters in porcelain and bone china. Along with the Industrial Revolution, there arose in England a "newly rich" bourgeoisie that demanded a supreme standard of elegance, richness, and comfort in their homes. The potters of porcelain and bone china catered to this market. As a result, we find examples of elaborate porcelains produced at the same time as some "cumbrous excesses of ill-planned ornament." There was no competition between these two branches of the pottery industry for, indeed, they had different goals.

The Great Exhibition of 1851, held outside London, had sixty-two exhibitors of china, porcelain, and earthenware. Most displays were colorful, beautifully painted, and lavishly gilded. In a contemporary essay describing the exhibition, R. N. Wornun wrote that "profusion of ornament is the rule." Ridgway, a Staffordshire potter, received an award and was praised for the "simplicity of the decoration." The 1851 *Art Journal* felt that the Ridgway exhibit was a refreshing novelty "amidst the jungle of riotous ornamentation." Today we occasionally locate a T.J. & J. Mayer stamp on white ironstone that, with the words "1851 Prize Medal," remind us that the humble potters exhibited, too.

White ironstone made in England and purchased in America, was popular from 1840 to 1870, but was sold less extensively after 1900. Beautiful in its simplicity and well adapted to the American way of life, this white ware has been absorbed along with the culture and language of England.

British accounts of ceramics have mostly overlooked the production of nineteenth-century white graniteware. The whiteware production had little to do with that "colossally self-confident and richly exhuberant artistic temperment that gave us great detailed architecture in the Victorian period."

Josiah Wedgwood, the best-known of the English potters in the last quarter of the eighteenth century, wrote about the general exporting of china: "Our consumption is very trifling in comparison to what is sent abroad...to the continent and the islands of North America. To the continent, meaning Europe, we send an amazing quantity of white stoneware and some of the finer kinds, but for the islands, meaning America, we cannot make anything too rich or costly."

Thus we perceive that this plain ware had no cultural or historical significance to English potters. In America, the story was different.

The early colonists were so busy wresting a living from the land, clearing their acres, and watching Indians that, except for the wealthy gentry, there was little time to be concerned with elegant table services. They used wooden trenchers, pewter dishes if they could be secured, and rough redware that was not dissimilar to our common flowerpots. The few potters labored diligently, making bricks and tiles for construction and shaping housewares such as pots, jugs, milk pans and crocks which were all too clumsy to import.

Wedgwood had noted that America was rich in all the resources necessary for making dishes. Especially during the periods when England and the colonies were waging wars, abortive attempts were made to produce simple tableware, but the American potteries did not flourish until the 1870s and 1880s. Perhaps the average citizen of this new and untried land was so concerned with the hills and valleys that stretched beyond the western horizon that he had no time to examine or shape the clay at his feet.

Therefore, when the potters from the Staffordshire area of England began to offer less expensive wares, the American housewife was a hungry customer. Many of the blue-and-white dishes, simply labeled Staffordshire wares today, were imported and eagerly purchased during the first half of the nineteenth century. By the late 1830s, those who worked with English clay had perfected an even more inexpensive, durable, and plentiful type of earthenware dish. Even the poorest of rural families gladly put away their wooden trenchers and redware to set their tables with spotless white.

Undoubtedly, it was in the hearts of many of these homes that the restless urge to go west originated. The earthenware could be packed easily and was tough enough to survive trail life. One of our ancestors writes that, from his home on the bank of the Mohawk River, the greatest break in the Appalachian Chain that stretches from Canada to Georgia, he could watch the covered wagons going up the valley "like ships under full sail." Loaded with the water jugs, the "bread loaf" trunks, the homespun blankets, and the churn, there must have been sturdy white ironstone.

In the pioneer homes that were built along the way, homemakers urged their frugal husbands to use a little of their year's profit to buy a set of dishes. Today, by looking in the homes of the pioneers' descendants, we can piece together a picture of that first treasured set.

President soap dish by J. Edwards, pitcher by John Alcock, and bowl by R. Beswick. Collection of Mr. and Mrs. John Black. Photograph: Black.

Octagonal shapes from four different potters. Photograph: Blair.

Punch and hot toddy cups. Top row, left to right: **Hyacinth, Ribbed Bud, Boote's 1851 Octagon, Curved Gothic.** *Bottom row, left to right:* **President, Fig, Sydenham, Arbor Vine.** *Photograph: Blair.*

Display of octagon-shaped pieces includes **Boote's 1851 Octagon, Fig, Sydenham, Gothic,** *and* **Baltic.** *White pitchers perch on high shelf. Photograph: LeBel*

2 Before White Ironstone

Working in earth makes men easy-minded.
—Staffordshire men

Nearly all of the English dishes we call ironstone were produced in the Staffordshire area of England, where materials were available and the port of Liverpool was a convenient distance to the north and west. Here, in the nine settlements of Tunstall, Longport, Burslem, Cobridge, Hanley, Stoke, Fenton, Lane End, and Longton, lived colonies of proud, capable potters. Other areas of England undoubtedly produced similar ware, but we seldom come across them in the United States.

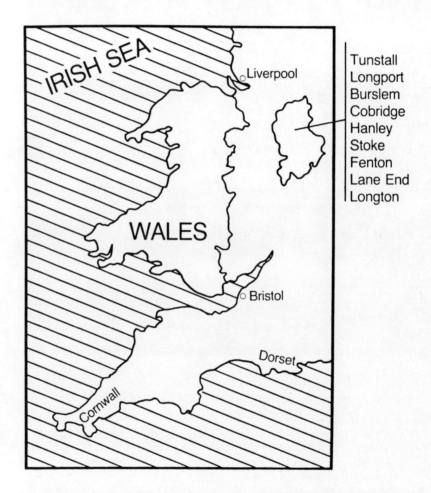

The great Josiah Wedgwood, who headquartered his pottery in Staffordshire, never made the durable wares we know as ironstone, but he certainly influenced its later production. He was interested in many fields other than the business of pottery and was aware of the forces at work in the countries and continents of the world. Wedgwood followed avidly the news that came back to England from her colonies across the wide Atlantic. Although he supported the causes of the American Revolution, he was still businessman enough to become concerned that his firm might lose its colonial market.

Eight or nine years before the War for Independence began, Wedgwood sent a Mr. Griffith to South Carolina to collect white clay, a fine white earth called "Ayoree" by the natives. The Cherokee Indians there had been making excellent pipes from the clay for years. Mr. Griffith brought back five tons of this clay, which was found to be fairly good quality. However, the Cornish clays were superior and could be had more simply and cheaply.

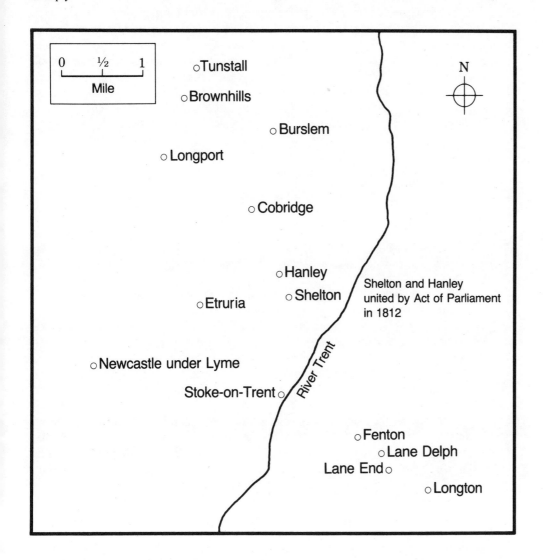

Wedgwood continued to voice his fear that able English potters would go to America and be lost to the English industry, but the Revolution kept the colonists so busy that no serious potteries were established. The white clays of the Cherokee lands were daubed with the blood of the battling colonists and the invading English. Meanwhile, the American housewives gladly drank their "liberty tea" from rough, molded redware cups. In reality, Wedgwood had little to fear, as the American Revolution destroyed all competition.

Surprisingly, the war was scarcely over when trade with England flourished again. The English merchants were eager to supply the American markets, and the new country had a hankering for goods that were too time consuming to manufacture themselves.

In 1768, William Cookworthy obtained an English patent that gave him the right to the sole use of *china clay* and *china stone* (see Chapter 4). Richard Champion took over the patent in 1774, causing a group of Staffordshire potters headed by Josiah Wedgwood to rise up in protest a year later. Champion was granted the use of the materials to manufacture transparent ware only. This opened a whole new field, for after this, any potter had the right to experiment with these materials in the potting of opaque china.

In 1784, Richard Champion left Bristol for North America and unsuccessfully experimented with the Cherokee clays. Attracted to the stretching acres, he settled on a plantation nearby, became a planter, and eventually filled several public offices. In this case, Wedgwood's fears of American rivalry proved groundless.

Wedgwood had produced a cream-colored ware called "Queen's ware." Then, in 1779, he first made "pearlware." This was not made in great quantity, but it is important as a "precursor of the durable white granite wares made later by such potters as Maddock, Meakin, and Grindley," according to the account written by Graham and Wedgwood. This, of course, was a reference to white ironstone. The whiter body was invented by increasing the proportions of china clay and flint and adding to the clay mixture a minute quantity of oxide of cobalt to neutralize the last traces of the yellow color. This operates on the same principle as adding bluing to brighten our laundry.

An interesting letter written by Wedgwood to his friend Bentley in 1787 attributes the improvement in white stoneware to the addition of calcined flint. He said:

> The *white stoneware* was produced by using the white pipe clay instead of the common clay of this neighborhood, and mixing it with flint stones calcined and reduced by pounding into a fine powder. The use of flint in our pottery is said to have proceeded from an accident happening to one of our potters, a Mr. Heath of Shelton, on his way to London. His horse's eye becoming bad, he applied to an hostler on the road, who told him he could cure the horse and showed him what means he used. Accordingly he took a piece of black flint stone and put it into the fire, which, to our potter's great astonishment, came out of the fire a most beautiful white, and at the same time struck him with an idea that this fine material might improve the stoneware lately introduced among them.

He brought some of the stones home with him, mixed them with pipe clay and made the first *white flint stoneware*.

Other authors, however, claim that Dwight of Fulhams used calcined, beaten and sifted flints in his wares fifty years earlier. Astbury is also claimed as inventor of this process (see Chapter 1).

Certainly, Josiah Wedgwood had a great influence on the pottery world. He was supportive of new ideas, he was the originator of mass production, and he developed worldwide markets.

We cannot leave the name of Wedgwood without mentioning his talented relative, Ralph. His pottery was not successful; he was ruined financially through losses during the Revolutionary War. His creative mind produced many new ideas, three of which were patented in 1796 and relate to the development of sturdy china. The first was a new, less costly method of "casing over inferior compositions commonly used for white ware." The second was a new glass-like finish created by adding alkaline salts or borax and calcareous earth. The third was an improved potter's oven, with fireplaces situated indoors instead of out. In the nineteenth century, Ralph turned to inventing in other fields.

Two events occurred in the last decade of the eighteenth century that hastened the development of new kinds of opaque china. Champion's patent had finally expired in 1796, and the Cornish materials became accessible for any purpose the potters required. In 1794, a high tariff had been imposed on imported porcelain. As a result, the Chinese trade slowed, and the English potters initiated experiments with new bodies.

Geoffrey Godden, in his *Godden's Guide to Mason's China and the Ironstone Wares*, advances a more logical explanation for the end of the importation of Chinese porcelain by the English East India Company. Tons of these porcelain dishes had been used in ships as "vital cargo, being both water resistant and heavy to make the vessels sailworthy." On top of this porcelain ballast, eighteen to twenty million pounds of tea each year traveled safely to England in the late eighteenth century.

The crates of inexpensive china were to be sold at bulk auctions to the English "chinamen." Godden quotes old records to prove that, in 1791, the directors of the East India Company "decided to cease their bulk importations of Chinese porcelains," because the china dealers were conspiring to cheat the importers.

The conspiracy was a familiar one—the practice of forming a pool or "ring" of buyers who agreed before an auction not to bid against each other, thus wrongfully lowering the sale price. Then the dealers would privately divide their items. The company was convinced in the 1790s that the chinamen had been systematically "fleecing" them for years. The china dealers were understandably concerned and objected vehemently, but the English East India Company had no more patience with the wily purchasers.

Meanwhile, china buyers looked elsewhere for new china sources, and potters experimented with new bodies to satisfy market demands. The production of new, durable stone chinas solved both of these problems.[1]

William and John Turner of Caughley were the first well-known potters to market an inexpensive, durable type of earthenware that could compete with the popular imported Chinese ware. It was composed of "New Rock" Cornish stone and prepared flint. The Turners' firm went bankrupt in 1806.

Josiah Spode II, from Stoke-on-Trent, manufactured a similar china. It was opaque, with a far finer texture than previous earthenware. It emitted a clear ring when lightly tapped, and its dense body was so fine that it resembled porcelain. The body of Spode's original version of felspathic ware had a delicate blue-gray tint. This color was to be repeated in the later mass-produced "felspar china," another name for ironstone. Spode called this ware "Stone China" at first; later, it was marked "New Stone."

Other potters, such as Davenport and Hicks & Meigh, marketed sets of china with a hard opaque body decorated to imitate the Chinese imports. There was a vast world market begging for this useful stoneware.

Working with his sons, Miles Mason of Lane Delph mastered a similar process. In 1813, his son, Charles James Mason, made public his "Patent Ironstone China." Although the product was not much different from the competitors', the name appealed to the buyers. Mason was a good huckster, and soon housewives on the continent and in America clamored for "ironstone" china. This new term became a permanent addition to the ceramic vocabulary.

Experts concede that the Rorstrand factory in Sweden was producing an admirable ironstone china, or *flintporslin,* as early as 1780. But we must not forget that it was the excellent Chinese imports with their brilliant glazes and hard bodies that prompted the English potters to innovate. They experimented in secret, produced their own special china bodies, and used good business practices to try to outsell their competitors. The abstract of Mason's July 1813 patent read as follows:

> A process for the improvement of the manufacture of English porcelain, this consists of using the scoria or slag of Ironstone pounded and ground in water with certain proportions, with flint, Cornwall stone and clay, and blue oxide of cobalt.

Mason's patent was granted for a period of fourteen years and was not renewed, probably because the other major potters had perfected their own ironstone bodies by 1827. In his book, *The Illustrated Guide to Mason's Patent Ironstone China,* Godden writes, "Several authorities have stated that the materials mentioned in the patent would not, on their own, make a workable ceramic body, and that the patent specification was a misleading front." At any rate, Mason has gone down in pottery history as introducing a durable, heavy earthenware called "Patent Ironstone China."

In his *Encyclopedia of British Pottery and Porcelain Marks,* Geoffrey Godden lists the potters of "Mason's Ironstone":

Blue hexagonal jug, an example of Mason's early ironstone, was a forerunner of the octagonal shapes that were to become so popular in white ironstone. Photograph: Blair.

G. M. & C. J. Mason	c. 1813 – 1829
Charles James Mason & Co.	c. 1829 – 1845
Charles James Mason	c. 1845 – 1848 and 1851 – 1854
Francis Morley (& Co.)	c. 1848 – 1862
G. L. Ashworth & Bros.	c. 1862 –

Beginning about 1810, ironstone was decorated with blue underglaze printing. Our ancestors loved to buy "Historic Staffordshire" china that attempted to picture places and events dear to growing America. It has been said that the sale of these deep-blue designs applied to white ironstone did more to heal the wounds caused by the War of 1812 than all the words of the great British and American leaders. In the twenty-five years following the conflict, dish-hungry America was flooded with mass-produced ironstone china decorated with cobalt blue. Wealthy citizens still preferred porcelain, but the blue-and-white earthenware was purchased eagerly by merchants and professionals. Soon these flow-blue dishes lowered in price so that poorer households were able to own a set. With the over-production though, some shoddy, poor quality pottery was produced.

Many of the cobalt blue pieces were not marked but can be attributed to certain potters by their border designs—a sort of prideful trademark. You may find marked plates from two different firms with the same center scene or design. The shrewd potters blatantly borrowed scenes from each other but left the borders to their originator. W. Adams circled his plates with baskets of roses and medallions; Wood used shells in his borders; Stubbs mixed eagles, scrolls, and flowers on the edges of his earthenware.

E. Wood & Co. potted the earliest known English blue and white earthenware, and Ralph and James Clews manufactured exceptionally beautiful flow-blue dishes from 1818 to 1838. (James came to the States in 1836 to venture unsuccessfully into the pottery business at Troy, Indiana.) Many authors have found the subject of these old blue dishes interesting and have written extensively about them. A few of their titles are listed at the end of this chapter.

The old blue dishes were decorated by transfer methods. Designs were kept uniform by using a die that was coated with color. A thin paper was pressed on the coated design, removed, and then placed on the area to be decorated. About sixty-five known artists depicted more than seven hundred subjects. The rich, dark-blue color is the most collectible today.

In the 1830s, the potters began using other colors, such as black, brown, green, red, pink, mulberry, and light blue. The purplish-brown mulberry and the light blue were employed most.

These tints were manufactured from the mid-1830s into the 1850s. The pattern name usually was printed on the back in a foliated or flowery cartouche. Often, an oval or oblong wreath-type mark was used.

The white ironstone about which this book is concerned first appeared in the same shapes as the dishes decorated with light blue transfers. Examples I have seen have been made from the same molds, but one is in plain white and the other is overlaid with a design in blue transfer.

The typical English potter was aware of the tastes of his prospective customers and was alert to new ideas that could be adapted to enhance his own products. Strong pottery families handed down their knowledge through generations and were unwilling to publicize their new discoveries. Perhaps that is why a potter like Mason was willing to patent a name and a recipe listing the wrong proportions. These potters produced thousands of white ironstone sets before the end of the century.

Relish dishes formed from the same mold indicate that the transition from transfer designs to plain white designs was a gradual process. Many Gothic designs are found decorated. Plain ones became more popular in the 1850s. Photograph: Blair.

Shortly after 1850, the Staffordshire firms felt threatened by the French potters who began exporting quantities of inexpensive hard, white porcelain to United States and Canada. The firms were afraid that housewives would prefer the glittering gray-white porcelains to the English transfer-colored earthenwares that had been so popular.

The crafty British potters took immediate steps to imitate the gray-white wares of the French, and the resulting tough, white earthenwares with sharp, detailed potting and gleaming glazes seized the American market. White ironstone with descriptions such as *a la perle, Parisian granite, Paris white,* and *porcelaine opaque* are reminders of this little international contest.

The poet James Torrington Spencer, describing a tour of the Staffordshire potteries in the 1860s, inspected the factory of T. & R. Boote in Burslem and talked of their "Granite or Opaque Porcelain, Otherwise Iron-Stone China." Other examples by ceramics historians prove that many names for this felspathic stoneware were interchanged, even as they were manufactured.

In succeeding chapters, you will become acquainted with the patterns and shapes of white ironstone that were so eagerly purchased by your great, great grandmother.

The following names have been used through the years to mark white ironstone china.

A la perle	Patent Paris white ironstone
Berlin ironstone	Patent ironstone china
Dresden opaque china	Pearl china
Felspar china	Pearl ironstone china
Felspar opaque china	Pearl stone ware
Fine stone	Pearl white granite
Flint ware	Pearl white ironstone
Genuine ironstone china	Porcelaine a la perle
Granite	Porcelaine opaque
Granite china	Quartz china
Granite ware	Real ironstone china
Imperial white granite	Real stone china
Imperial granite	Rock stone
Imperial ironstone china	Royal granite
Imperial Parisian granite	Royal ironstone china
Imperial stone	Royal patent ironstone
Improved granite china	Royal patent ware
Improved ironstone china	Royal premium
Improved stone china	Royal stone china
Indian ironstone	Royal vitreous
Ironstone china	Staffordshire ironstone china
Ironstone pearl china	Staffordshire stone china
New stone	Staffordshire stone ware
Opaque china	Stone china
Opaque granite china	Stone granite
Opaque porcelain	Stone ware
Opaque stone china	Superior stone china
Oriental stone	Warranted stone china
Parisian granite	White granite
Parisian porcelain	White granite ware
Paris white	

References to Explore

Camehl, Ada Walker. *Blue China Book.* New York: Dutton, 1916.

Coysh, A.W. *Blue-printed Earthenwares.* Rutland, Vermont: Charles E. Tuttle Co. Inc., 1972.

Klamkin, Marian. *American Patriotic and Political China.* New York: Crown Publishers, Inc., 1969.

Larsen, E. B. *American Historical Views on Staffordshire China*. New York: Doubleday & Doran, 1939. Reprinted by Dover Publications, 1979.

Little, W. L. *Staffordshire Blue*. New York: Crown Publishers, Inc., 1969.

Willis, N. P., author, and Bartlett, William H., illustrator. *American Scenery*. London: Virtue, 1838.

3 Mastering the Marks

How can you estimate the age of an ironstone dish? Was it English or American made? Is it an original or a reproduction? With a magnifying glass, a little study, and much handling of old dishes, you can become quite knowledgeable.

Beware of overconfidence, however. The English potters interchanged finials on different patterns or sometimes just made a new handle if it was more expedient. Examples of this are the three variations of the *Atlantic Shape*, small changes in the *Sydenham Shape* pitchers, the absence of the rope trim on some *Ceres Shape* covers, the two differently shaped soap dishes of the *Fig* pattern, and the horizontal and the vertical toothbrush holders found in *Ceres Shape* toilet sets. I've had to retract some of my broad generalizations so I've practically banished the words "always" and "never" from my ironstone vocabulary. Saves me a lot of embarassment.

You will soon be able to recognize an old piece by its blue-white color. The later English wares and the American-made pieces look creamy white when set next to the old English dishes.

STAFFORDSHIRE KNOT	ROYAL ARMS	GARTER

Godden's Encyclopaedia of British Pottery and Porcelain Marks lists some general rules for reading the marks on the bottom of dishes potted during the nineteenth century.

"Any printed mark incorporating the name of the pattern may be regarded as subsequent to 1810."

"Use of the word 'Royal'. . .suggests a date after the middle of the nineteenth century."

"Any printed mark incorporating the Royal Arms (or versions of the Arms) are 19th century or later."

"The quartered Arms without the central inescutcheon are subsequent to 1837."

"Many 19th century marks are based on stock designs-variations of Royal Arms, a garter-shaped mark (crowned or uncrowned) or the Staffordshire knot."

"The garter-shaped mark was used from 1840 onward. The Staffordshire knot may occur from about 1845. . .much used in 1870s and 1880s. . . ." (It was not used extensively on white ironstone.)

Printed marks became popular after 1800 and were applied either before or after glazing. Impressed marks were made by applying a metal die to the dish before the first firing. This is generally referred to as "impressed under glaze." This type of mark usually is found on older pieces of china. However, many of the older pieces had only the black printed mark, while some had both impressed and printed marks. You may have to use your magnifying glass to search for impressed letters around the rim of the base of a gravy boat, vegetable dish, or open compote.

Applied marks were more rare. They were actually impressed marks placed on a raised pad. The potter formed them separately from the rest of the dish and, before firing, adhered the potter's identification on the base with a little slip. This type of mark was used by S. Bridgwood & Son and Richard Alcock. Elsmore & Forster used it on such patterns as *Ceres, Morning Glory,* and *Laurel Wreath.* Other examples undoubtedly can be found.

By American law, the word *England* had to be affixed to imported goods after 1891. Some potters, however, had proudly marked their wares *England* before the law was passed, so the collector will have to become acquainted with the few potters who did this. An example is the firm of J. & G. Meakin, who began labeling dishes with *Burslem, England,* as early as 1869.

Made in England is a twentieth-century dating. *Limited, LD., Ltd.,* etc. indicate that a piece was made after the 1860s, but they were not generally used before the 1880s. *Trade Mark* followed the Trade Mark Act of 1862. Usually it referred to a date after 1875.

Much ceramic ware produced between 1842 and 1883 bore a diamond-shaped registry mark either printed or impressed on the bottom of a dish. Employed to prevent design piracy, this "bundle" contained the original design filed at the Patent Office. The date recorded when the design was introduced and was not necessarily the date the item was potted. The protection lasted for an initial period of three years, so the mark is a guide in dating. The marks generally related only to the shape and the impressed design. As a result, don't be surprised to find a *Copper Tea Leaf* or other colored decoration over a design that had already been potted in plain white. A chart of the letters, numbers and their interpretation follows.

Index to Year and Month Letters

Years

1842-67					1868-83				
Year Letter at Top					Year Letter at Right				
A	=	1845	N	= 1864	A	= 1871	L	=	1882
B	=	1858	O	= 1862	C	= 1870	P	=	1877
C	=	1844	P	= 1851	D	= 1878	S	=	1875
D	=	1852	Q	= 1866	E	= 1881	U	=	1874
E	=	1855	R	= 1861	F	= 1873	V	=	1876
F	=	1847	S	= 1849	H	= 1869	W	=	Mar. 1-6
G	=	1863	T	= 1867	I	= 1872			1878
H	=	1843	U	= 1848	J	= 1880	X	=	1868
I	=	1846	V	= 1850	K	= 1883	Y	=	1879
J	=	1854	W	= 1865					
K	=	1857	X	= 1842					
L	=	1856	Y	= 1853					
M	=	1859	Z	= 1860					

Months
(Both Periods)

A = December
B = October
C or O = January
D = September
E = May
G = February
H = April
I = July

K = November (and
December 1860)
M = June
R = August (and
September 1st-19th,
1857)
W = March

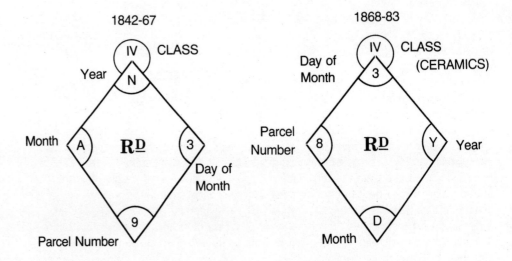

From 1884 on, designs were registered by numbers as listed below:

Rd. No. 1–Jan. 1884
19754–Jan. 1885
40480–Jan. 1886
64520–Jan. 1887
90483–Jan. 1888
116648–Jan. 1889
141273–Jan. 1890
163767–Jan. 1891

185713–Jan. 1892
205240–Jan. 1893
224720–Jan. 1894
246975–Jan. 1895
268392–Jan. 1896
291241–Jan. 1897
311658–Jan. 1898
331707–Jan. 1899

If the number is above 360,000 the date is after the year 1900. A few of the early white ironstone patterns *(Rose Bud, Line Trim,* and *Gothic)* were marked with a patent number and were also marked with the diamond-shaped registry, suggesting an earlier system of numbering patterns.

The word *warranted* nearly always designated American work, but here again, the rule does not always prove true. For instance, the English potter John Edwards often marked his late-nineteenth-century dishes with the words *Warranted Ironstone China,* and Anthony Shaw marked his later pieces *Stone China Warranted.* Yet, I repeat, the addition of *warranted* occurred most often in American ironstone marks. If you are in doubt, check to see if the potter's name is included in the list of English potters of white ironstone found in this book. If not, you probably are holding an American-made dish. Occasionally a dish is found that gives the name of an English potter and, underneath, is marked *made for* with the name of an American retailer beneath.

Each ironstone collector seems to have a pattern that he *just knows* was called *Pearl.* I'm no exception. When I investigated, I found the word *Pearl* included again and again in the marks of nineteenth-century English potters. Remember that the famous Josiah

Wedgwood made his ''pearlware'' in 1779. Later potters may have been attempting to ''borrow'' a little of his success.

I've seen *Pearl* marked on the underside of several patterns by J. Wedgwood, in the marks of the several potters of the *Wheat and Clover* pattern, on *Scotia Shape* by F. Jones & Co., on dishes by G. Phillips, W. Baker & Co., T. Walker, J. & G. Meakin, and others. Godden's *Encyclopaedia* confirmed my research with the words ''*PEARL WARE* or *PEARL STONE WARE:* Name for special earthenware body, used by many nineteenth century firms. Impressed or incorporated in printed marks.''[3]

Some marks simply say *Pearl*, while others refer more directly to the bodies with descriptions such as *Pearl China*, *Pearl Stone*, *Pearl Ironstone China*, and *Pearl White Ironstone*. Below are a few examples copied from white ironstone dishes:

T.J.&.J. Mayer and its subsequent firms (Mayer Bros. & Elliot, Mayer & Elliot, and Liddle, Elliot & Son) sometimes included the mark *Berlin Ironstone*, which was a name for the ironstone body used. This has caused some people to think this the name of a pattern, but it was printed on many different patterns.

A few kind manufacturers impressed the potting date into the body of the clay itself. Davenport marked the last two digits of the year on either side of his famous anchor. Such firms as Liddle Elliot & Son impressed two numbers, one above the other, denoting the month and year of the potting. For example, $^{11}/_{63}$ means November 1863. A few of the later potters simply impressed the last two digits of the year in a spot separate from the more familiar mark.

The well-known ''prince of potters,'' Josiah Wedgwood, contributed much to the development of white ironstone, as has been discussed elsewhere in this book. His descendants produced a ''Stone China'' from about 1827 to 1861, with limited production, and marked it ''Wedgwood's China'' (a rare marking). However, the Josiah Wedgwood firm manufactured and usually labeled their excellent and beautiful wares simply ''Wedgwood.''

The inexpensive white ironstone sent to the United States in the nineteenth century was not made by this illustrious family.

Podmore, Walker, & Wedgwood of Tunstall marked their wares:

P. W. & W.   WEDGWOOD OR WEDGWOOD & CO.

Godden remarks that it was advantageous to use the name Wedgwood alone. From about 1860, the firm was retitled, Wedgwood & Co., and it continued as Wedgwood & Co. Ltd. until 1965, when the name was changed to Enoch Wedgwood, Ltd. Some of the marks collectors can attribute to this company are the following:

after 1862

Several familiar patterns, such as *Fig, Corn and Oats,* and *Sharon Arch* are marked J. Wedgwood. These pieces have been assigned to John Wedge Wood, since the Josiah Wedgwood potteries did not use marks with the initial "J." Sometimes the marks of John Wedge Wood have a slight gap or dot between "Wedg" and "Wood." These marks have been traced to John Wedge Wood:

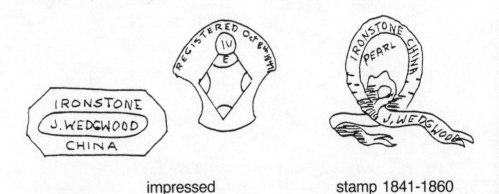

impressed   stamp 1841-1860

These uses of the Wedgwood name undoubtedly were intended to confuse consumers. This problem plagued the Wedgwood potters for generations. Misleading marks stamped on other types of pottery through the years have been "Wedgewood," "Vedgewood," and "Wedgwood Ware"—all wares inferior to the Wedgwood standards. If the renowned Wedgwoods ever acknowledged the inexpensive white ironstone that influenced American life, I have never been able to find an example. White ironstone potters have contributed to the Wedgwood puzzles.

Nevertheless, I have heard antique dealers proudly proclaiming, "It was made by Wedgwood," and I have been as guilty as they in adding magic and value because of a name. I hope the poor Josiahs (there were five of them) have not been too bothered by the misuse of that great Wedgwood label.

Potters Whose Marks Have Been Found on
White Ironstone Made in England in the Nineteenth Century

	Location	Dates of Operation
Adams, Wm. & Sons	Tunstall, Stoke	1796 - present
Alcock, Henry & Co.	Cobridge	1861 - 1910
Alcock, John	Cobridge	1848 - 1861
Subsequently Henry Alcock & Co.		
Alcock, John & George	Cobridge	1839 - 1846
Alcock, John & Samuel	Cobridge	1848 - 1850
Alcock, Richard	Burslem	1870 - 1882
Alcock, Samuel & Co.	Cobridge	1828 - 1853
Ashworth, Geo. & Bros.	Hanley	1862 - present
Baker, W. & Co.	Fenton	1839 - 1932
*Barrow & Co.	Longton	1853 - 1856
Bates, Elliott & Co.	Longport	1870 - 1875
Beswick, R.	Longton	?
Bishop & Stonier	Hanley	1891 - 1939
Bodley, Edward F. & Co.	Burslem	1862 - 1898
Boote, T. & R.	Burslem	1842 - 1906
Bourne, Joseph	Denby	1833 - 1860
Bowers, George Frederick	Tunstall	1842 - 1868
Bridgwood, S. & Son	Longton	1805 -
Bridgwood & Clarke	Burslem, Tunstall	1857 - 1864
Subsequently Edw. Clarke & Co.		
**Brougham & Mayer	Tunstall	1853 - 1855
Brownfield, Wm. & Sons	Cobridge	1850 - 1891
Burgess, Henry	Burslem	1864 - 1892
Burgess & Goddard	Longton	c.1870
Burgess & Meigh	Burslem	1867 - 1889
Challinor, Charles	Tunstall	1848 - 1865
Challinor, C. & Co.	Fenton	1892 - 1896
Challinor, Edward	Tunstall	1842 - 1867
Challinor, E. & Co.	Fenton	1853 - 1862
Subsequently E. & C. Challinor		
Challinor, E. & C.	Fenton	1862 - 1891
Clarke, Edward (& Co.)	Tunstall	1865 - 1877
	Longport	1878 - 1880
	Burslem	1880 - 1887
Clementson Bros.	Hanley	1865 - 1916
Clementson, Joseph	Hanley	1839 - 1864
Close & Co.	Stoke	1855 - 1864
Cockson & Chetwynd (& Co.)	Cobridge	1867 - 1875
Subsequently Cockson & Seddon		
Cockson & Seddon	Cobridge	1875 - 1877
Collinson, C. & Co.	Burslem	1851 - 1873
Cork & Edge	Burslem	1846 - 1860
Cork, Edge, & Malkin	Burlsem	1860 - 1871
Corn, Edward	Burslem	1840 - 1860
Corn, W. & E.	Burslem	1864 - 1891
	Longport	1864 - 1904
Davenport	Longport	1793 - 1887
Edge, Malkin & Co.	Burslem	1871 - 1903
Edwards, James	Burslem	1842 - 1851
Edwards, James & Son	Burslem	1851 - 1882
Edwards, John (& Co.)	Longton	1847 - 1853
	Fenton	1854 - 1900

Edwards, T.	?	?
Elsmore & Forster	Tunstall	1853 - 1871
(Sometimes Forster was spelled "Foster")		
Ford & Challinor	Tunstall	1865 - 1880
Forester & Hulme	Fenton	1887 - 1893
Furnival, Jacob (& Co.)	Cobridge	1845 - 1870
Furnival, Thomas (& Sons)	Cobridge	1851 - 1890
Furnivals (Ltd.)	Cobridge	1890 - 1968
Gator, Thomas & Co.	Burslem	1885 - 1894
Gelson Bros.	Hanley	1868 - 1875
Goodfellow, Thomas	Tunstall	1828 - 1859
Goodwin, John	Longton	Prior to 1851
See Seacombe Pottery		
Goodwin, Joseph		
Hancock, Sampson (& Sons)	Tunstall	1858 - 1870
	Stoke	1858 - 1937
Harvey, C. & W.K.	Longton	1835 - 1853
Heath, Joseph	Tunstall	1845 - 1853
Holland & Green	Longton	1853 - 1882
Hollinshead & Kirkham	Tunstall	1876 - 1890
Hope & Carter	Burslem	1862 - 1868
Hughes, Thomas	Burslem	1860 - 1894
Hulme, T.		c. 1855 -
Hulme & Booth	Burslem	1851 - 1854
Johnson Bros.	Hanley	1883 - present
Jones, Frederick & Sons	Longton	1865 - 1886
Jones, George	Burslem	c. 1854
Jones, George & Sons	Longport	1861 - 1951
Liddle, Elliot & Son	Longport	1862 - 1870
Livesley & Davis	Hanley	?
Livesley, Powell & Co.	Hanley	1851 - 1866
Maddock, John	Burslem	1842 - 1855
Maddock, John & Sons	Burslem	1855 - present
Maddock & Gater	Burslem	1874 - 1875
Malkin, R.	Fenton	1863 - 1881
Mason, Charles James	Fenton	1845 - 1848
		1851 - 1854
Maudesley J. & Co.	Tunstall	1862 - 1864
Mayer, Thomas & John	Longport	1841 - 1843
Mayer, T.J. & J.	Burslem	1843 - 1855
Subsequently Mayer Bros. & Elliot		
Mayer Bros. & Elliot	Burslem	1856 - 1858
Subsequently Mayer & Elliot		
Mayer & Elliot	Longport	1858 - 1861
Subsequently Liddle, Elliot & Son		
Meakin, Alfred	Tunstall	1875 - present
Meakin, Charles	Hanley, Burslem	1883 - 1889
Meakin & Co.	Cobridge	1865 - 1882
(Meakin Bros.)		
Meakin, Henry	Cobridge	1873 - 1876
Meakin, J. & G.	Hanley	1851 - present
Meakin, Lewis	Shelton	1853 - 1855
Meigh, Charles	Hanley	1835 - 1849
Meigh, Charles & Son	Hanley	1851 - 1861
Meigh, Charles, Son & Pankhurst	Hanley	1849 - 1851
Meikle Bros.	Liverpool	?
Meir, John & Son	Tunstall	1837 - 1897
Mellor, Taylor & Co.	Burslem	1880 - 1904

Morley, Francis (& Co.)	Hanley	1845 - 1858
Old Hall Earthenware & Co.	Hanley	1861 - 1886
Pankhurst, J.W.	Hanley	1850 - 1851
Pankhurst, J.W. & Co.	Hanley	1852 - 1882
Pearson, Edward	Burslem	1850 - 1854
Pearson, Edward	Cobridge	1853 - 1873
Phillips, George	Longport	1834 - 1848
Pinder, Bourne & Co.	Burslem	1862 - 1882
Pinder, Bourne & Hope	Burslem	1851 - 1862
Podmore, Walker & Co.	Tunstall	1834 - 1859
Subsequently Wedgwood & Co.		
Powell & Bishop	Hanley	1876 - 1878
Powell, Bishop & Stonier	Hanley	1878 - 1891
Proctor, John	Longton	1843 - 1846
Ridgway, Bates & Co.	Hanley	1856 - 1858
Ridgway, John & Co.	Hanley	1830 - 1855
Ridgway & Morley	Hanley	1842 - 1844
Ridgway, Wm. & Co.	Shelton	1830 - 1854
Ridgway, Wm., Son & Co.	Hanley	1838 - 1848
Seacombe Pottery	Seacombe	1851 - 1870
	(near Liverpool)	
Shaw, Anthony	Tunstall, Burslem	1850 - 1882
Shaw, Anthony & Son or Sons	Tunstall, Burslem	1882 - 1898
Shaw, Anthony & Co.	Tunstall, Burslem	1898 - 1900
Taylor, W.	Hanley	?
Till, Thomas & Sons	Burslem	1850 - 1928
Turner, Goddard & Co.	Tunstall	1867 - 1874
Turner, G. W. & Sons	Tunstall	1873 - 1894
Turner & Tomkinson	Tunstall	1860 - 1872
Venables & Baines	Burslem	1851 - 1853
***Venables, John	Burslem	1853 - 1855
Walley, Edward	Cobridge	1845 - 1856
Walker, Thomas	Tunstall	1845 - 1851
Wedgwood & Co.	Tunstall	1860 - present
Formerly Podmore, Walker & Co.		
(& Wedgwood)		
Wedgwood, J.		
(*See* John Wedge Wood)		
Wilkinson, Arthur J.	Burslem	1885 - 1964
Wilkinson & Hulme	Burslem	1883 - 1885
Subsequently Arthur J. Wilkinson		
Wood & Hulme	Burslem	1882 - 1905
Wood, John Wedge	Burslem, Tunstall	1841 - 1860
Printed mark "J. Wedgwood"		
Wood & Son(s)	Burslem	1865 - present
Wood, Son & Co.	Cobridge	1869 - 1879
Wood, Rathbone & Co.	Cobridge	c. 1868
Wooliscroft, George	Tunstall	1851 - 1853
Also spelled Woolliscroft	Tunstall	1860 - 1864

Scottish Potters

Bell, J. & M.R. & Co.	Glasgow	1842 - 1929
Cochran, Robert & Co.	Glasgow	1846 - 1918

Irish Potters

Belleek Pottery Ltd.	Belleeck	1863 - present

| South Wales Pottery | Llanelly | 1839 - 1858 |

Made a "Pearl White Ironstone"

Adriatic pieces by Barrow bear an 1850 mark.
**Collectors report earlier marks.

***This firm also traded as Venables Mann & Co.

The English coat of arms found on many sets of white ironstone (both from Staffordshire and America) bore two mottoes. Sometimes both were included. Most often printed around the quartered shield were the words *Honi soit qui mal y pense,* meaning "Evil to him who evil thinks." Supposedly, this is based on a remark made by King Edward III when he put on a garter lost by a countess who had been dancing with him. Some historians discount this as an amusing tale.

Frequently found below the coat of arms royal lion and mythical unicorn was a draped ribbon inscribed with the saying, *Dieu et mon droit,* which means, "God and my right." Thus, the arms of Britain, with many minute variations, proclaimed that the manufacturers were English.

4   The Potter's Craft

The making of pottery is the most ancient craft still practiced by mankind, with the exception of designing weapons. Primitive man, comfortable with the idea that he was related to the "dust of the earth," had respect for the clay under his feet. Clay vessels, such as earthen bowls used for storing, cooking, and drinking, have preserved the story of civilization.

Toward the close of the seventeenth century, the northern Staffordshire area of England, located to the south and east of the port of Liverpool, became a pottery center. The settlement of Burslem had already been nicknamed the "butter pottery" because it potted so many butter crocks. The British government was concerned that the use of so much wood had depleted the forests, and it encouraged the use of alternate sources of heat. Thus, pottery families were attracted to the Staffordshire area, where there were plentiful deposits of coal and large beds of suitable clay.

The best and most original earthenware ever designed in England was executed by such Staffordshire potters as Elers Bros., Astbury, Josiah Wedgwood, Wheildon, and Woods during the first half of the eighteenth century. These leaders were not trying to imitate the wares of other countries, as did future potters.

This creative English upsurge of strong earthenware production ceased when England finally uncovered the secret of making porcelain, and the earthenware designers tried to adapt their methods for manufacturing porcelain. The ceramics historian Henry Sandon writes, "It took England a long time to discover how to make porcelain, many years of striving to produce a white translucent ware to equal the Chinese."[1] English porcelain was truly beautiful by the end of the 1700s.

Even though many factories felt that they had finally arrived, most firms "made pedestrian wares for cheaper, competitive purposes." This was a perfect description of the ironstone wares so eagerly purchased by the European middle class and the china-hungry Americans in the nineteenth century. This highly vitrified earthenware was made from felspathic stone rocks that fuse at great heat. The resultant body is so dense and strong that the term "ironstone" was fitting.

The most common body, *China Stone,* consisted of Dorset or Poole clay, kaolin from Cornwall or Devonshire, and flint. This was the same body described by the French as *petuntse,* relating to the materials used in the Chinese wares. Petuntse literally means "little white bricks." Appropriately, the prepared material was stored in the shape of bricks.

A better body, *China Clay,* the whitest, purest form of clay, was made of the same ingredients, except that the Dorset or Poole clay had been produced by the decomposition of granite. This was the beginning of the general term *white granite,* which used to describe both English and American white ironstone.

Cookworthy of Cornwall has been credited with discovering the correct proportions of clay, kaolin, and flint. Each substance had its own preparation. The Dorset or Poole clay, the chief ingredient, was mixed with water, passed through sieves of different sizes, cleared of lumps, and finally rendered to a fine consistency. The kaolin needed no cleaning. The flints were used as they came, passing through grinding mills until reduced to minute particles in water, then drained. This combination of materials made up the China Stone or China Clay.

The China Stone was calcined or burnt in kilns, crushed, and reduced to fine powder in mills. Then it was ready to be used.

The proportions were different for different wares. Water was mixed with the prepared elements, and the resulting mixture was taken to the slip-kiln, a long brick trough heated by flues from a furnace. There the mixture was kept simmering, evaporating the water until a doughlike substance emerged. If the potter desired a whiter product, cobalt oxide was then added to the mixed clay. This potter's clay was stored in a cold, dark cellar until needed.

Molds had been used in making white salt-glazed products, and their use continued into the age of ironstone. Before 1730, plates and bowls were formed by taking a "bat" of clay and pressing it into or on a mold. It was difficult to make the ware thin enough with this method. The first molds were cut from Derbyshire alabaster, using a difficult skill learned by the "block cutters." By the mid-eighteenth century, molds were being made from porous plaster of Paris. Often they were made in two or more pieces that were later fastened together.

The potter took his clay out of storage, added enough water to make a thick slip, and poured it into a mold. He let the material stand a few minutes while the mold absorbed some of the water, then he poured off the superfluous slip. Because clay tends to shrink as it dries, the potter could easily remove the loose mold from the thin clay casting, which was now ready for drying. Casted shapes were dried before being kiln-baked.

The kiln or oven was fired until the proper heat was reached. The fire was continued for three days. A kiln fired on Monday was ready "to be drawn" (to have the saggers removed) on Friday morning. The pottery at this stage was known as *biscuit*—fired but not glazed.

The lead glazes were discontinued on tablewares because they were toxic. The salt glazes were easy to apply (just cast salt into the kiln filled with forms), but the resultant pottery had a pitted finish undesirable in table services. An excellent felspar glaze was perfected, but because it included expensive borax, it was used only on costly services until after the early 1830s. The principal ingredient was felspar, which had been ground to a fine powder. The published recipe, which was not patented and remained free to all, was "27 felspar, 18 borax, 4 Lynn sand, 3 nitre, 3 soda, 3 Cornwall china clay." This was melted to a frit and ground to a fine powder with three parts of calcined borax added before grinding. As far as I can ascertain, the tough glaze on white ironstone was made from similar materials.

Varying according to the potter, the materials of the glaze were mixed with water to the consistency of cream. The biscuit earthenware was skillfully dipped into this creamy solution. The water sank into the porous body until a thin coating of the pulverized glaze remained. Then the dish was placed in a *glost kiln* for one day. The glost kiln was subjected to less heat than the biscuit kiln; there was just sufficient heat to reduce the coating to a layer of glass. This glaze hindered the access of liquids to the unprotected earthenware beneath. There must be a close relationship between the fusing point of the body and the glaze that covers it. If not, checking or crazing occurs sooner.

Small pieces, such as decorations or handles, were often forced into *thumb molds,* with the pressure of the thumb. Intricate pieces were made in parts from separate molds, then the parts were joined with a little slip and were all fired as one unit. The thick slip was merely potter's clay mixed with a little water. It was applied much as a housewife uses water to attach an extra piece of pie crust.

The Edwards dish shown was probably molded in six pieces; the body of the bowl, the cover, the two handles, the gourd finial, and the hollow base ring.

After shaping, the forms were taken to special drying rooms. Here much of the water content was lost, which facilitated future handling.

When dry enough, the pieces were placed in large flat-bottomed pans, either oval or round, with vertical sides. These were called *seggars* or saggers and were constructed of refractory materials, such as fire clays, broken earthenware, broken saggers, or damaged clays. The forms were packed as closely as possible. The saggers were arranged one above the other in a kiln, which often was shaped like a beehive in the earlier days.

The saggars were covered so that soot and ashes from the flue would not damage the wares. Occasionally, we find edges that seem to be "peppered" under the glaze. These are on pieces of china that were not sufficiently protected in the biscuit kiln.

Six or seven plates or bowls were stacked in the saggers and separated by three-pronged *stilts* or *spurs*. These pieces of baked clay left three marks on the back and inside of some pieces. Sometimes pegs were inserted in holes inside the saggers, and rims of dishes rested on these supports. Today, the signs are visible on the finished articles.

These are the processes by which ambitious Staffordshire potters produced set after set of gleaming blue-white dishes and chamber sets for the homes of America.

5 What's in a Set?

Collectors of white ironstone are always excited when they locate a piece that was used for an unusual purpose. Services made from the 1840s through the 1860s had many more pieces than those assembled after 1870.

An 1827 sale list included these pieces as parts of a set of dishes: two soup tureens with covers and stands, six sauce tureens with covers and stands, four vegetable dishes with covers, nineteen dishes in various sizes (platters or relish dishes?), two fish plates, sixty table plates, eighteen soup plates, and forty-eight pie plates.

Without seeing a complete set, we can only speculate about what it looked like. Certainly the sixty table plates must not have been all the same size. And why aren't cups listed? One of our dear old neighbors, who is more than ninety years young, remembers that his mother had two sets of "wheat ironstone," which she used during harvest meals for hop pickers. Do you suppose this could have been one enormous set similar to the one described above?

Plates were made in these five sizes: 10½" dinner plate, 9½" dinner plate, 8¼" luncheon plate, 7¼" pie plate, and 6¼" bread and butter plate. Often, shallow soup plates were made in an enormous 10" size, a normal 9" size, and the more rare and collectible 7½" server. In addition, two desirable little plates available are the 4" cup plate and the deeper 4¼" to 5¼" honey dish. This last piece is sometimes big enough to be used for a saucedish.

The large soup tureens, complete with cracker tray and ladle, were exactly copied in the little sauce tureens. Some sets, such as *President Shape,* have the great oval soup tureen as well as the large round chowder tureen. They both have trays and ladles. The same round shape is duplicated in miniature in the smaller round sauce tureens, too.

Most early ironstone offered two shapes of covered vegetable tureens. Each shape came in small, medium, and large. Examples include *Boote's 1851 Octagon* in pedestalled octagon servers with no handles, and the rarer handled octagonal tureens with no pedestals; the *Sydenham* in round tulip servers and the rarer oval tureens with spectacular finials; and the *President* with both oval and round covered tureens. Large, low tureens that have an opening for a ladle have been nicknamed stew tureens by collectors.

Treasured are the high compotes (sometimes called comports) and the low doughnut or cookie stands found in some patterns.

Open, elongated octagonal, rectangular, and oval servers in various sizes were called *bakers.* Don't try to bake in them, though! Early sets sometimes contained a nest of six or seven round, low bowls that measured from 8" to 14" in diameter. It's not surprising that I have never seen a collection with all sizes. Do not confuse these nests with the later square and round ribbed sets of the 1870s and 1880s, which can be easily found.

Morning Glory fruit dish, 2½" high and 11¼" in diameter, is from the collection of James and Doris Walker, New York. Photograph: Blair.

Twiffler or twyfller? The term refers to nineteenth-century china. It is usually defined as a "middle-sized plate" or a "muffin plate." In 1842, a "twiffle-maker" was described as "a maker of small plates." Seen any twifflers lately?

The most common white ironstone cup was a teacup made without handles and was similar to oriental tea bowls. This style was cheaper to pot and more apt to survive ocean voyages intact. These handleless cups came in two sizes: a 7½ oz. teacup with a 6″ saucer, and a 10 oz. coffee cup with a 6½″ saucer. Rarely, we locate the same cups with handles, so we must suppose that some cups were ordered with handles.

Other cups include shaving mugs, the unusual large cider mugs, handled and handleless demitasse cups, handled 4″ punch or hot chocolate cups, the shorter handled hot toddy cups, and the popular miniature cups with saucers.

*White ironstone cups. Top row, left to right: Handleless demitasse cup, Edward's **Lily of the Valley** shaving mug, **Bordered Hyacinth** cider mug, **Twin Leaves** coffee cup, **Fig** syllabub cup. Bottom: Handled and handleless **Sharon Arch** teacups and miniature **Sharon Arch** cup with saucer. Photograph: Blair.*

***Victor Shape** tea set minus the sugar bowl, by F. Jones. Photographed from the collection of Mr. and Mrs. Gary Grove, Pennsylvania.*

Tea sets included a teapot, sugar and creamer, waste bowl, six cups with saucers, and dessert plates. Dinner sets contained at least four relish dishes shaped like leaves, boats, or shells. This is reminiscent of the early-nineteenth-century colored breakfast or dessert services.

True butter dishes are difficult to track down because most of them did not survive. Many that have been located are brown and stained with an accumulation of butter fat. Even after professional cleaning, these dishes may turn brown once more. Although I usually urge collectors to use their ironstone, I make an exception with butter plates, unless you can find a plastic liner to fit!

Platters seem to have survived better than most white ironstone dishes. The largest turkey platters are about 16" by 20". Other meat platters vary in sizes, with the smallest about 12" long. Most desirable, but difficult to locate, are the large well-and-tree footed platters with separate perforated liners. Occasionally, we come across a long, narrow fish platter.

Teapots and coffeepots were manufactured. The coffeepots were larger, holding three or four more cups than the teapots. Sugar and creamer sets came in two sizes in some patterns such as *Sydenham* and *President Shapes*.

The jugs (pitchers) for these early services came in large and small creamers, three sizes of table beverage pitchers, and two sizes of ewers from toilet sets. They form a great parade as they march along an old pine cupboard shelf.

One of the few butter dish survivors, potted by John Edwards in **President Shape.** *Photograph: Groff. Collection of the Dalenbergs.*

Sydenham *pitchers from 5" to 12¾" high. There are slight differences in some borders. Collection of Mr. and Mrs. James Walker. Photograph: Blair.*

Rare **Ceres** *muffin or covered hotcake server by Elsmore & Forster. Collection of Dick and Adele Armbruster. Photograph: Groff.*

Pewter lidded syrup dispenser. Mark illegible. Photograph: Blair.

We can't leave this subject without raving about a few pieces that ironstone detectives covet. The first is one of the pewter-lidded ironstone syrup dispensers. Collectors long to own a covered hot beverage jug. Can you spot the four depicted in this book? I watched for years for the covered hotcake server or muffin dish. I had accumulated three bottom halves of these servers in *Ceres, Boote's 1851 Octagon,* and *Tuscan Shape.* At long last, I came across the *Ceres* treasure depicted here. It is 9¾″in diameter, with scallops inside the bowl. The cover rests on top of the plate, which has no indentation for the lid.

The miniatures usually were not made for children, but were fashioned carefully and then distributed to dealers as models of the large services. Today, we call them "salesman's samples." Not all patterns were copied in miniature. The fact that we see recurring pieces of the same patterns suggests that only certain shapes were molded for this method of advertising.

Here is a list of some of the different miniature shapes that collectors have described again and again: *Ceres Shape, Boote's 1851 Octagon, Panelled Grape, For-get-me-not, Edward's Lily-of-the-Valley, Sharon Arch, Prairie Shape, Burgess' Lily Shape, Boote's Prairie Flower,* and a Meakin set decorated with strawberries. I have never seen these last two patterns in a normal size. Also included here is a drawing of a Pankhurst set with arched panels that are topped by a lily. In a later chapter, you'll find pictures of the simple miniature sets potted in America in the 1880s.

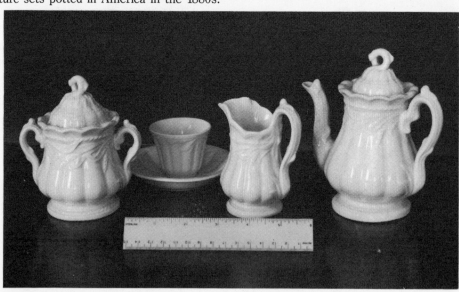

Ceres *miniature tea set by Elsmore & Forster. Rare, clearly marked. Owners are John and Jane Yunginger from Minnesota. Photograph: Blair.*

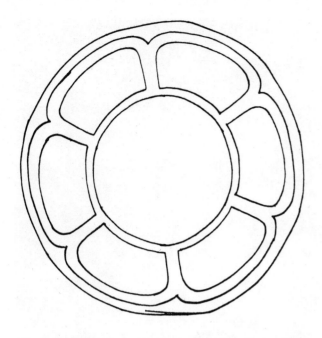

Nineteen out of twenty white ironstone collectors still search for a beverage bowl. Smaller handleless syllabub bowls hold 2½ to 3½ quarts; the covered and handled hot toddies are usually a little larger and often are bought and used without the cover. I've seen only two of the large, 6- to 8-quart punchbowls. I still dream of the great scalloped edges on the beautiful proportions of the *Adriatic Shape* in the large punchbowl.

Hot beverage jugs (sometimes called hot chocolate pitchers) do not have a hole in the lid for ventilation as do teapots. The cover is rather pointed over the lip; there is definitely a rim for the cover. These have been seen in *Boote's 1851 Octagon, Gothic, Tiny Oak and Acorn, Prize Bloom,* and *New York Shape.*

A complete toilet set was composed of ewer and basin, covered soap dish, horizontal brush holder, covered chamber pot, and shaving mug. Sometimes there was also a waste container or a foot bath. These last two pieces are hard to find and command higher prices if they were potted before 1870.

Burton, in his *The Georgians at Home*, suggests that the horizontal brush holders may first have been used as a holder for "toothsticks," ancestors of our toothbrushes. A home recipe read "lemon juice, mixed with burnt alum and salt, rubbed on a clean rag, wrapped around the end of a stick."

Boote's 1851 Octagon Shape *hot beverage jug is uncommon in that there is no hole for ventilation and the cover is elliptical on one side. Lucky owners are John and Jane Yunginger, Minnesota. Photograph: Blair.*

Waste jar (missing lid) in **Panelled Columbia.** *Collection of Ray and Priscilla Casavant. Photograph: Groff.*

Edward's **Fluted Panels** *on a foot bath (rare) from a toilet set discovered by Carl Groetzinger. Photograph: Wetherbee.*

After 1870, English firms offered fewer pieces in their white ironstone services. Except for some of the plain white, cups were seldom sold without handles. Saucers often had high walls. Butter chips, bone dishes, occasionally egg cups, and individual saucedishes or little platters were added. Most sets contained one or two tureens plus open servers. Soup tureens became much smaller and almost disappeared from sets by 1890. Butter dishes with perforated liners above a space for ice were made regularly. Many of these were similar to the earlier round soap dishes that had been a part of the mid-century toilet sets. Cup plates and honey dishes were no longer part of dinner services. Sauce tureens were rarely made by that time, but the gravy boat remained popular. Nested round or square bowls and the earlier waste bowl shapes (with a new function) were freely used and can be picked up easily today. Some 16 oz. chowder cups are occasionally found.

In the late 1800s, the more affluent industrial class began to refer derogatively to the inexpensive, useful white wares as "thrasher's china." It is true that the rural folks gladly continued to use these plain, practical dishes long after the majority of Americans had purchased colored porcelains to set their tables.

This detailed listing of various pieces of white ironstone should be a real challenge to collectors. There is still much available for the hunter.

6   The Launching of White Ironstone

A few pieces of white ironstone can be traced to the late 1830s, but most potters did not produce these simple dishes until the 1840s and 1850s. The hexagonal and octagonal bodies that already had been the bases for colored transfer designs were used at first. The *Primary Shape* and especially the *Gothic Shape*, familiar from the 1830s, were seen again in basic white.

PRIMARY
SHAPE

Primary Shape

James Edwards of Burslem probably created a wider range of patterns than any other Staffordshire potter of the 1840s. Shortly after the Great Exhibition of 1851, T. J. & J. Mayer potted its *Prize Bloom* and *Prize Puritan*, each proudly marked Prize Medal.

Both J. Wedgwood and Davenport produced the pattern *Scalloped Decagon*. In later chapters, you'll see that the same two potters marked other shapes *Fig*, *Fig Variation*, *Sharon Arch*, and *Corn and Oats*. Somehow there is a story here. Great cooperation? Piracy? All of these shapes are registered. And all these introductory patterns are eagerly accumulated by ironstone collectors.

Gothic chowder tureen with plateau liner and ladle, registered by T. J. & J. Mayer in 1847. It dwells in a corner of an old country restaurant, Saltzman's Hotel, Ephratah, New York. The 5½" creamer by James Edwards was also registered in 1847 with accompanying No. 44036. Photograph: Blair.

James Edwards' creamer, hot beverage pot, and sugar bowl in **Gothic Shape.** *Photograph: Blair.*

Gothic *teapot and covered tureen, both by John Alcock. Photograph: Wetherbee.*

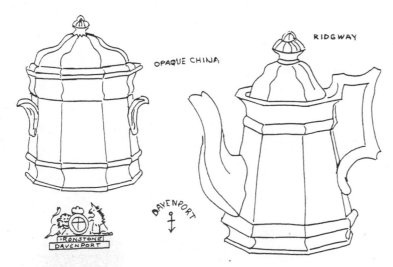

Gothic, an early pattern used by many different potters in the 1840s and 1850s. Some makers were the Mayers, Ridgway, Davenport, and James Edwards.

Gothic Shape *carafe made by J.F. Collection of Doris and James Walker, New York. Photograph: Blair.*

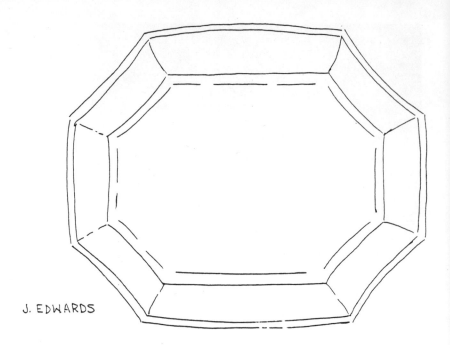

J. EDWARDS

Curved Gothic by James Edwards, registered 1843, the earliest diamond-shaped registry mark that I have seen on white ironstone.

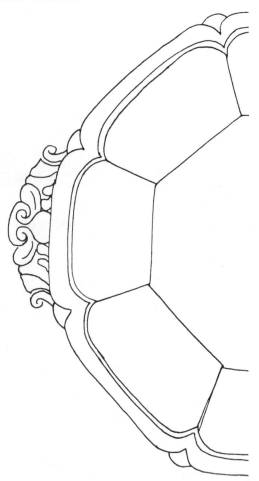

Bordered Gothic by T. Walker, John Alcock, others.

Curved Gothic epergne, 14" tall. "Manufactured for E. A. & S. R. Tilley, St. Louis, Mo. by T. J. &. J. Mayer, Longport," on bottom. Owned by Mr. and Mrs. John Black, New York. Photograph: Blair.

Gothic Cameo tureen registered in 1847. This same cameo motif was used on mulberry and blue transfer china made by John Alcock, James Edwards. Photograph: Blair.

Gothic Rose. C. Meigh & Son.

Close-up of cameo head below handle of **Gothic Cameo** *tureen.*

Berlin Swirl. T. J. & J. Mayer and their successors, Mayer & Elliott, and Liddle, Elliott & Son all made this popular pattern. A soup tureen manufactured by the first firm above was marked 1845, while the plate at left was impressed 1864. It was unusual for a design to be used for so many years.

Berlin Swirl relish dish by Liddle, Elliot & Son, and **Berlin Swirl** *cover, unmarked. Photograph: Groff.*

Small **Berlin Swirl** *punchbowl by T. J. & J. Mayer. Collected by Jane Diemer. Photograph: Diemer.*

J. EDWARDS

Line Trim J. Edwards, also G. Wooliscroft.

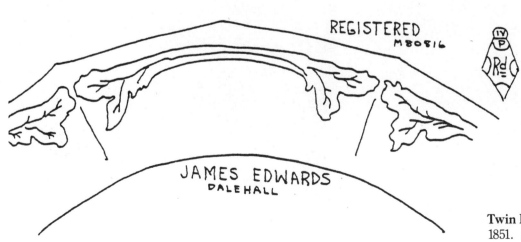

REGISTERED
M80816

JAMES EDWARDS
DALEHALL

Twin Leaves. James Edwards, registered 1851. An unusually heavy ironstone set with softened octagonal lines. The sugar bowl is hexagonal with a rosebud finial.

39

Scalloped Decagon. Davenport, registered 1853, but potted in 1856 as proved by the numbers on either side of the well-known Davenport anchor. J. Wedgwood also used this design.

Scalloped Decagon, *a design potted by both J. Wedgwood and Davenport. Creamer and large ewer from a toilet set owned by Mr. and Mrs. John Black. Photograph: Black.*

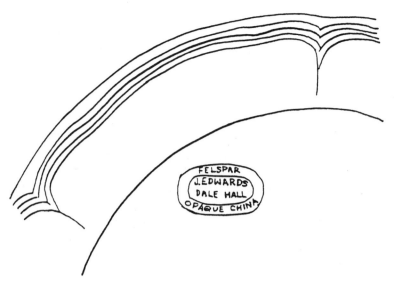

Triple Border. J. Edwards, an early design that has been reproduced by several modern factories.

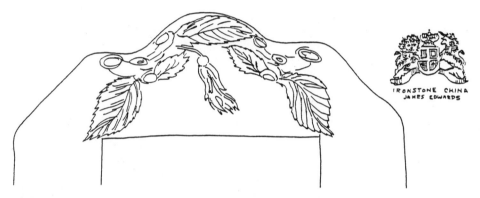

Rose Bud. James Edwards, marked in an unusual manner with No. 56632 and the additional words "Registered Dec. 16th, 1848 by James Edwards." This pattern is square, with flat, beveled corners. The covers are capped with big rosebuds.

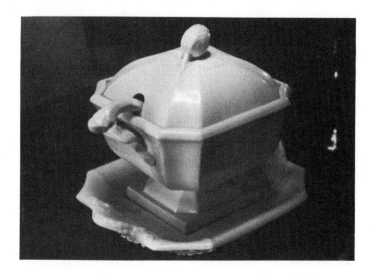

Square soup tureen with liner and ladle, registered in 1848 by James Edwards. The square corners appear to be cut off, and a large rosebud is the finial shape. Collection of Mr. and Mrs. William Horner. Photograph: Dr. Horner.

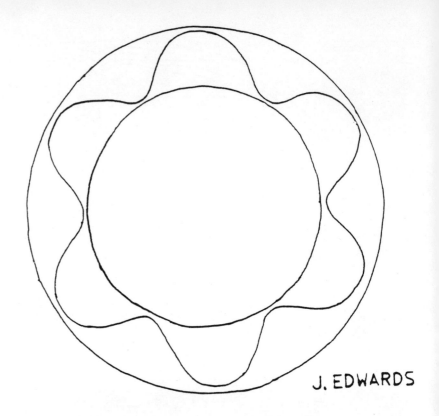

Rolling Star. J. Edwards. This is an unusual plate, with three-dimensional planes forming the curves.

Two James Edwards' pieces, a **Rolling Star** *platter and the* **Rose Bud** *gravy boat. Photograph: Blair.*

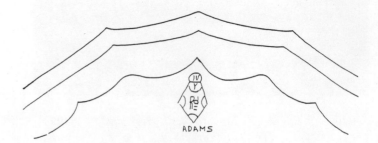

Adam's Scallop. William Adams, registered 1853.

Adam's Scallop tureen, 11" long with cone finial, registered 1853. Photograph: Blair.

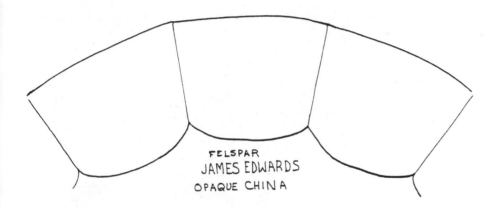

True Scallop. James Edwards, E.&C. Challinor.

Fluted Pearl pattern by J. Wedgwood, marked with diamond-shaped registry and "registered 1847." Collection of James and Doris Walker. Photograph: Blair.

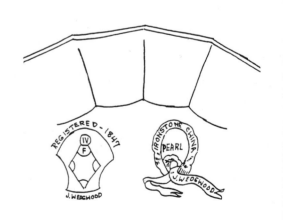

Fluted Pearl. J. Wedgwood, clearly dated 1847.

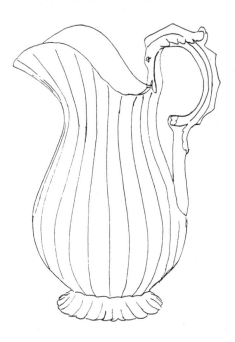

Fluted Pearl *vegetable tureen by John Wedgwood was used by Mrs. Adin Van Wie to serve her husband's beef stew. Photograph: LeBel.*

Coral Shape by J. Wedgwood, similar to **Fluted Pearl,** same potter.

Sauce tureen and ewer from toilet set in **Coral Shape** *by J. Wedgwood. From display in Museum of Texas Handmade Furniture, New Braunfels, Texas. Photograph: Bridges.*

Prize Puritan *by T. J. & J. Mayer, registered 1851.*

Prize Puritan *gravy boat by T. J. & J. Mayer. Collection of Ray and Priscilla Casarant. Photograph: Groff.*

Four-piece sauce tureen in **Split Pod** *by James Edwards. Collection of Howard and Dorothy Noble. Photograph: Groff.*

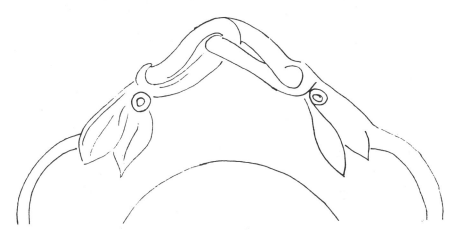

Split Pod. James Edwards pitchers were octagon shaped with vertical panels that were alternately convex and concave.

Prize Bloom *by T. J. & J. Mayer. A hexagonal shape with twelve concave panels and an extraordinary flower finial. Registered in 1853, owned by Mr. and Mrs. John Black. Photograph: Black.*

Prize Bloom *teapot from the collection of James and Doris Walker. Photograph: Walker.*

Enviable hot chocolate pot by T. J. & J. Mayer in the beautiful **Prize Bloom.** *Collection of Ray and Priscilla Casavant. Photograph: Groff.*

J.F. potted this uncommon **Walled Octagon.** *Photograph: Blair.*

Tiny **Panelled Acanthus** *creamer is unmarked. Photograph: Groff.*

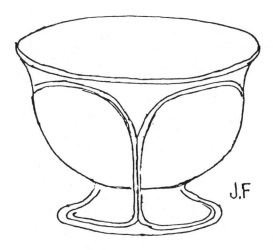

Quartered Round. J.F. Unusually small eggnog bowl.

Clean-lined **Panelled Octagon** *water jug by Elsmore & Forster from the early years of their 1851-1871 potting efforts. Photograph: Groff.*

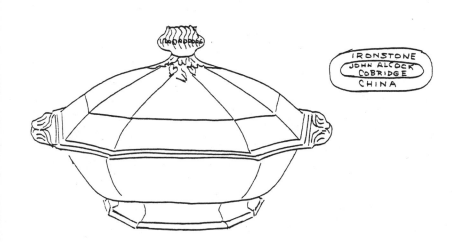

Long Octagon. John Alcock.

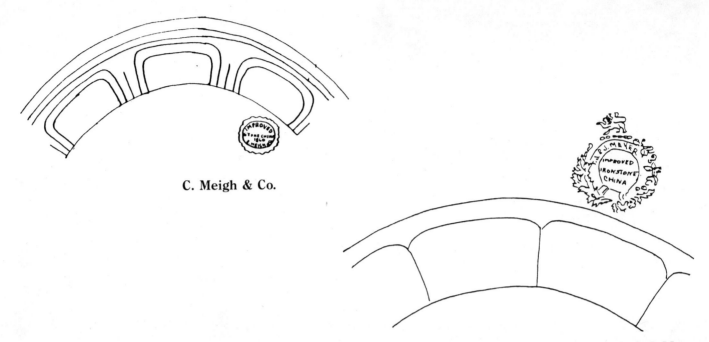

C. Meigh & Co.

T. J. & J. Mayer

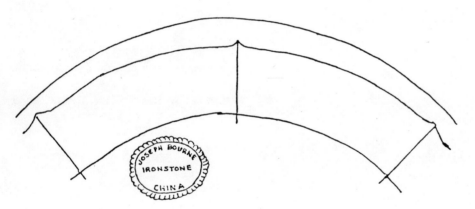

Joseph Bourne.

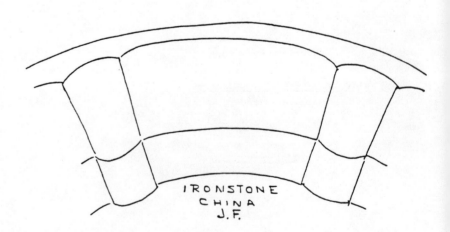

7 Sydenham Shape and Its Imitators

In the mid-nineteenth century, T. & R. Boote offered for sale to American homes an entirely new ironstone pattern. It was beautifully potted, with a gleaming surface that even today remains uncrazed and unstained. The lines were graceful and well-balanced. And the simplicity, in the midst of Victorian over-decoration, was a welcome relief. Even though collectors have long been hoarding precious *Sydenham* pieces, these dishes come to light regularly, suggesting to us that many services of this popular pattern found passage to America.

In 1842, Thomas and Richard Boote purchased the Waterloo Pottery and other works in Burslem and there perfected a new method of making floor tiles. They also have been credited with the introduction of the Parian wares. Their first ironstone services were presented at mid-century. These proved so popular that other potters promptly adapted similar shapes and related motifs to their own bodies.

Collectors and dealers alike call the earlier *Boote's 1851 Octagon* pattern by the name *Sydenham*. Though closely related, these are definitely two separate patterns. All *Boote's 1851 Octagon* pieces are marked with the 1851 registry, with the T. & R. Boote name on the bottom. *Sydenham* dishes, including the covers, are clearly stamped with the name of the pattern.

Covered vegetables dishes in *Sydenham* include three sizes of round servers with upward, sweeping lines resembling a tulip. They also had three sizes of oval tulip-like servers with magnificent finials. None of these had handles. A "nest" of a half dozen round, low, open dishes from 8″ to 14″ in diameter were potted.

A collector in southern New York owns a dozen leaf-shaped relish dishes, in which she serves individual salads. I also have seen the tall, flower-like fruit compote. I have never seen a punch or hot toddy bowl in *Sydenham,* but the Bootes must have produced them since we locate the "orphan" cups so often.

Occasionally, we find pieces that are lesser in quality molded and marked *Sydenham* by J. Clementson.

Boote's 1851 Octagon Shape, forerunner of the famous Sydenham Shape. Platter and baker are 12″ long. Photograph: Blair.

Boote's 1851 Octagon ring-handled teapot and covered vegetable tureen. Photograph: Dollard.

In 1850, the Bootes put up a new factory, in which they shaped the first pattern of the heavier *Sydenham* types. This has been simply nicknamed *Boote's 1851 Octagon Shape,* as taken from the registry date and lines. It was the forerunner of the now famous *Sydenham Shape*. The *Octagon* had a simpler border with deeper dishes and also introduced the ring-handled teapots.

Boote's 1851 Octagon milk jug, handleless coffee cup, and miniature cup and saucer. Photograph: Dollard.

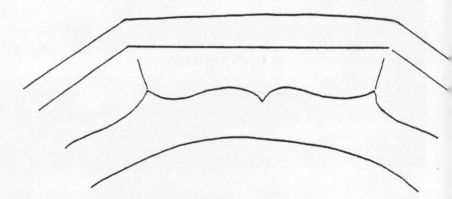

Boote's 1851 Octagon. T. & R. Boote, registered 1851. Plates repeat motif ten times. Round plates crowded the motif twelve times.

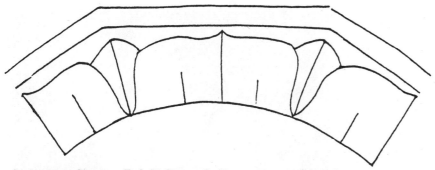

Sydenham Shape. T. & R. Boote, J. Clementson, registered 1853. Octagonal plates repeated motif ten times, but the round plates repeated motif eight times.

Echoing many of the *1851 Octagon* lines, the Bootes brought out their *Sydenham Shape* in 1853. They registered it again with small changes in 1854.

Just why the name *Sydenham* was chosen is unknown. It was the name of an old English family. Joseph Clementson and his partner, Reed, also made dinnerware for the American markets at a Hanley firm called The Sydenham Works. Clementson marked a flow-blue pattern by this name before white ironstone became popular. In 1851, there was a great fair held in a suburb of London named Sydenham. Perhaps one of these facts influenced the choice of the name.

Many sizes of *Sydenham* plates were manufactured in both octagonal and round shapes, from large 10″ plates down to tiny 4½″ cup plates. Platters and open vegetable servers, called bakers, were potted in oval or long octagonal lines. These bakers came in many sizes, varying from a generous, 12″ size down to a 7″ size.

The motif on sugar bowls, pitchers, handleless cups, and the pedestalled syllabub cups depicted the elongated leaf folded back over the vertical panels.

Desirable **Sydenham** *teapot by T. & R. Boote, accompanied by a box soap dish in* **Atlantic** *by Boote, and a toddy cup in* **Primary Shape.** *Photograph: Blair.*

High **Sydenham** *compote by T. & R. Boote is coveted by many Boote collectors. It is 10¾" in diameter and 7¾" high. Collection of Dick and Adele Armbruster. Photograph: Armbruster.*

Sydenham Shape *sugar bowl, creamer, and 10" plate by T. & R. Boote. Probably the most collectible pattern, with beautiful octagonal lines. Collection of James and Doris Walker, New York. Photograph: Blair.*

Sydenham Shape *soup tureen, complete with liner and ladle, is flanked by matching sauce tureens. All of the pieces in this remarkable grouping are from the collection of Mr. and Mrs. John Black. Photograph: Black.*

Sydenham *oval tureen, 12", discovered in the china closet of Saltsman's country restaurant in the historic Mohawk Valley. Photograph: Blair.*

Tulip Sydenham *serving dishes, characterized by sweeping upward lines. The J. F.* **Grand Loop** *gravy boat is used here to show how certain lines of this pattern influenced later designs. Photograph: Blair.*

Sydenham *toilet set offered by Boote. Here is a complete marked set, except for the mug and the subsitute cover on the chamber (an* **1851 Octagon***). These prizes are placed beside an old spool bed in the home of James and Doris Walker, who live in the foothills of the Adirondack Mountains. Photograph: Blair.*

In 1855 and again in 1856, Edwards registered his *President Shape*. Both oval and round shapes were used in the serving dishes, with varied finials and foliage for each.

The simple, squatty *President* pitchers and teapot have six vertical rounded panels, each grooved in the center and ending near the neck, with the same curves impressed on the plates. Pauline Meissen-Helter described "a large oval fruit bowl with a pedestal base and big embossed oak leaves spreading to each side of the body from closed scrolled handles."

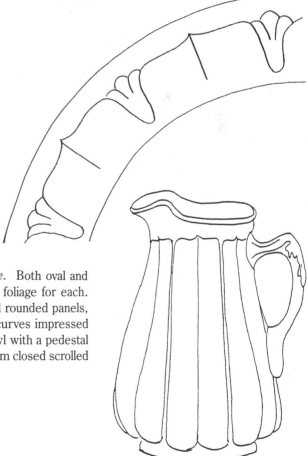

President Shape. J. Edwards, registered 1855 and again in 1856. Both round and oval shapes were used in serving dishes.

President *oval serving dish by John Edwards uses decor similar to the* **Sydenham Shape.** *Collection of Karl and Linda Dalenberg, Massachusetts. Photograph: Blair.*

President Shape *syllabub or toddy bowl, 3½ quart, with matching cups. The bowl is owned by the Blacks in New York, and the Dalenbergs in Massachusetts own the cups. Photograph: Black.*

Another related pattern registered in 1855 was marked with four different names. J. Clementson called his *Dallas Shape.* T. Hulme, J. Meir, G. Bowers, and G. Wooliscroft labeled their round and octagonal plates *Baltic Shape.* E. Pearson, a Cobridge potter, stamped his *Mississippi Shape.* And a jug identical to Pearson's has been seen marked *Maltese Shape,* E. Corn, Burslem.

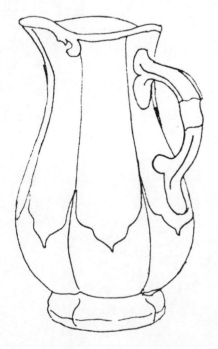

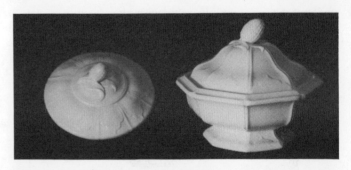

Probably either **Mississippi** *or* **Maltese Shape.** *The mark is blurred. The tureen is owned by the Casavants. Photograph: Groff.*

E. PEARSON

Mississippi Shape. E. Pearson, registered 1855. **Maltese Shape,** E. Corn (same pitcher).

Dallas Shape. J. Clementson, registered 1855.

Baltic Shape. T. Hulme, J. Meir, G. Bowers, G. Wooliscroft, registered 1855. Plates were made in both round and octagonal shapes.

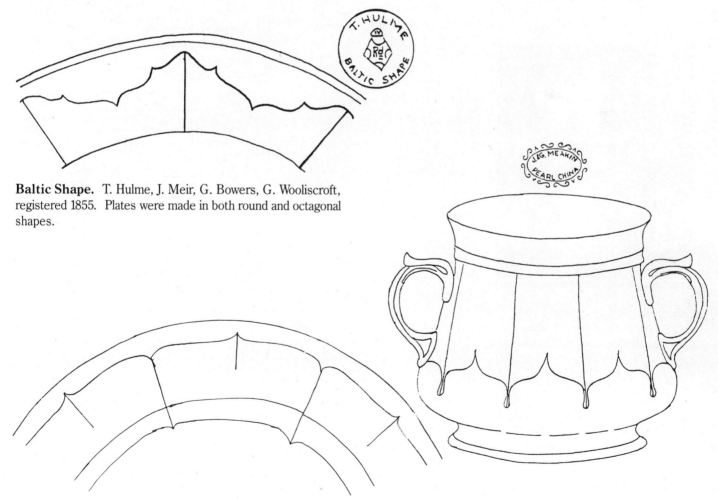

Pearl Sydenham. J. & G. Meakin. Usually uncrazed, gleaming white surfaces.

In my first ironstone handbook, I asked the question, "Can anyone write me if the company name is legible on your *Columbia* prize?" The response was surprising. Ironstone fans hastened to educate me by telephone and letters complete with photographs and drawings. The following potters of *Columbia Shape* have been verified many times over: Livesley & Powell, J. Clementson, E. & C. Challinor, Wooliscroft, J. Meir & Son, Penman Brown & Co., W. Adams, and Elsmore & Foster. I thought the first few collectors were unable to copy letters correctly on this last spelling, until I ran into "Foster," instead of "Forster" clearly impressed on three different pieces. Since I can find no record of such a firm, I wonder if the stamp was in error. The *Columbia Shape* was registered in 1855.

Mark taken from a **Columbia** sauce tureen.

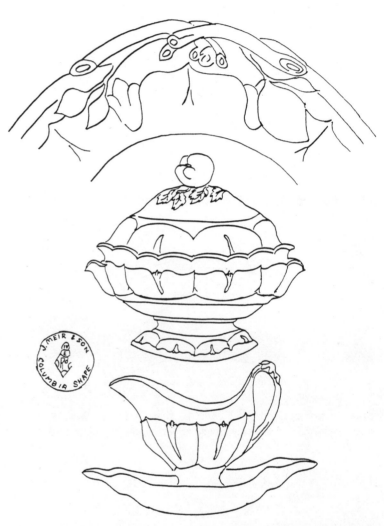

Columbia Shape sauce tureen with applelike fruit decoration. Owned by James and Doris Walker, New York. Photograph: Blair.

Columbia Shape. Livesley & Powell, J. Clementson, E. & C. Challinor, G. Wooliscroft, J. Meir & Son, and Elsmore & Foster (not Forster), W. Adams, Penman Brown & Co., registered 1855.

The design around the *Columbia* plates is more deeply impressed than in the *President*. Otherwise the two plate patterns are exactly the same except that the center line in the leaves of the *Columbia* is slightly split at the end. Note that detail in the border of the round sauce tureen.

Each *Columbia* potter used the same border on the plates and platters. Their originality was evident in the varied finials and foliage decorations. Notice the pod finial chosen by E & C. Challinor to grace their soup tureen. Watch closely, because you'll see the same finial used on other patterns.

Columbia Shape *soup tureen by E. & C. Chalinor, 15" long and nearly 13" tall, with a large pod finials.* Sydenham *cup and saucer included. Both from the collection of James and Doris Walker, New York. Photograph: Blair.*

Columbia Shape *well-and-tree platter with perforated liner is a rare piece and was potted by Clementson. Owners are Mr. and Mrs. William Horner. Photograph: Dr. Horner.*

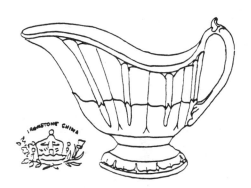

Panelled Columbia. Some of the pieces marked Columbia have vertical panels above the familiar border. Some are unmarked, others say "ironside china," and a Livesley & Powell mark is verified.

Unmarked Panelled Columbia *teapot. Photograph: Dollard.*

Uncommon syrup pitcher in **Panelled Columbia,** *unmarked. Photograph: Groff.*

Panelled Lily. Marked J. F. This dish echoes the shape introduced by the **Sydenham Tulip** in their vegetable servers.

PERSIA
SHAPE
E. CORN
BURSLEM

Persia Shape. Edward Corn.

Syrup dispenser in **Sydenham**-*type design. Sugar bucket, 12½". The dark stains inside suggest its use to serve "long sweetening," the syrup that was as black as molasses. Collection of Mr. and Mrs. John Black, New York. Photograph: Black.*

Double Sydenham. Anthony Shaw, Livesley & Powell & Co.,
T. Goodfellow.

Wrapped Sydenham. W. E. Corn, Anthony Shaw.

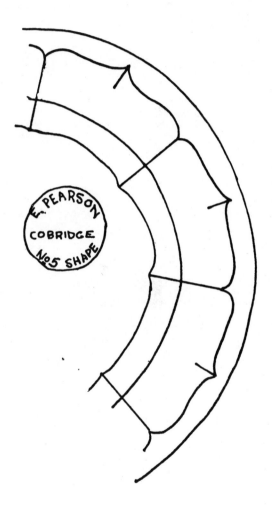

E. Pearson **No. 5. Shape.**

8 Notable Names

About 1850, some Staffordshire potters began to mark their new patterns with a stamped or impressed mark, which included a registry date, the name of the pottery firm, and for the first time, the name of the shape.

In 1850, Wedgwood & Co. (not Josiah) marketed white ironstone dishes labeled *Erie Shape*. The only *Erie* piece I have seen was a plain platter with no embossed decoration. Perhaps the finials and handles were original enough to warrant this special christening.

The same year, Barrow & Co., who only potted for a few years in the early 1850s, registered an original set clearly marked *Adriatic*. The finials were molded like a reclining sheaf of wheat topped by another upright sheaf. I once saw a large punchbowl in this shape with spectacular scallops around the top edge.

These two patterns, closely followed by the popular Boote's *Sydenham Shape* in 1853, were early examples of Staffordshire potters naming white ironstone shapes after well-known people or places.

T. & R. Boote followed their big success with such patterns as *Grenade, Union, Chinese,* and *Atlantic*. Because most early Boote pieces are still unstained, unchipped, and unchecked, they are especially desirable today. This firm did not usually include pattern names in their marks after 1870.

Most English potters of the 1850s named their sets, possibly because earlier flow-blue sets that depicted American scenes had wooed the American market. Thus we find dishes marked *Washington, Columbia, President, Mississippi, New York,* and *Virginia* among others. Naturally, Americans were eager to purchase a pattern named after their own state, so the connotations helped arouse interest in new sets advertised by the china merchants.

I have seen a *Kansas Shape, Pacific Shape,* and *Augusta Shape*. The *Augusta* plate had embossed scallops near the outer edge and a copper lustre band. It was marked *J. Clementson*. In 1871, the last year the firm of Elsmore & Forster manufactured, they marked sets *Pacific Shape*. The *Pacific* sugar bowl was completely covered with narrow concave ribs slanting straight up from a base larger than the shoulder. It was topped by a ribbed cover with a plain acorn finial.

The chapters on Sydenham-type shapes and on harvest decorations also include patterns that were named in the backstamp.

Adriatic finial.

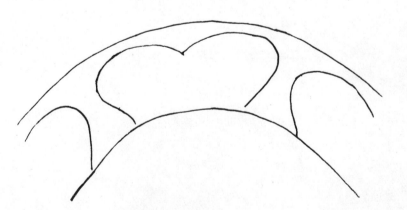

Adriatic Shape. Barrow & Co., registered 1850.

Barrow & Co. topped this large vegetable tureen in **Adriatic Shape** *with a sheaf of wheat. Photograph: Groff.*

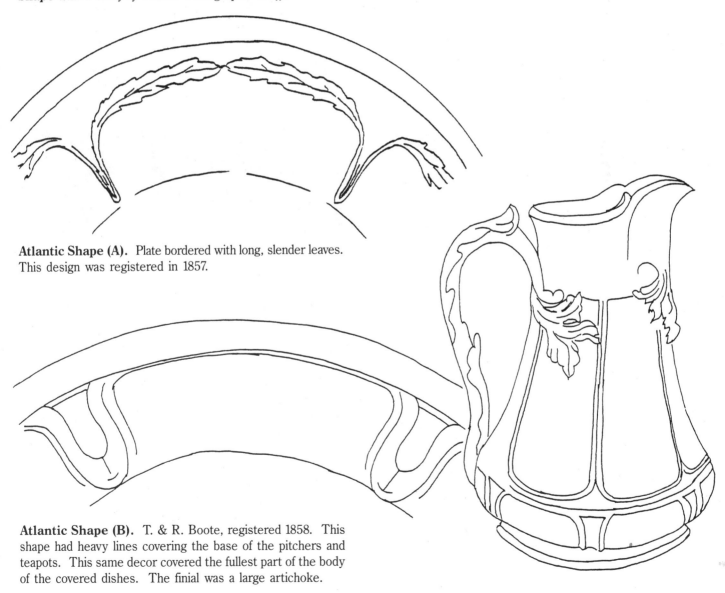

Atlantic Shape (A). Plate bordered with long, slender leaves. This design was registered in 1857.

Atlantic Shape (B). T. & R. Boote, registered 1858. This shape had heavy lines covering the base of the pitchers and teapots. This same decor covered the fullest part of the body of the covered dishes. The finial was a large artichoke.

Atlantic Shape (B) vegetable tureen by T. & R. Boote has a little petticoat under the body. *Photograph: Groff.*

Atlantic Shape (C). T. & R. Boote, registered 1858. The base of the beverage servers were ringed with large thumbprints. The plate motifs had added foliage. A round bud perched on top of the covers.

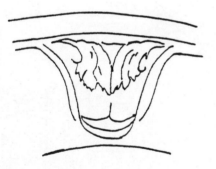

Boote's **Chinese Shape** tureen.

Atlantic Shape (C) by Boote. This used the same handle and leaves under the spout as the B shape, but the spout was squared, the base had large thumbprints, and the finial was formed as a bud. *Collection of James and Doris Walker. Photograph: Blair.*

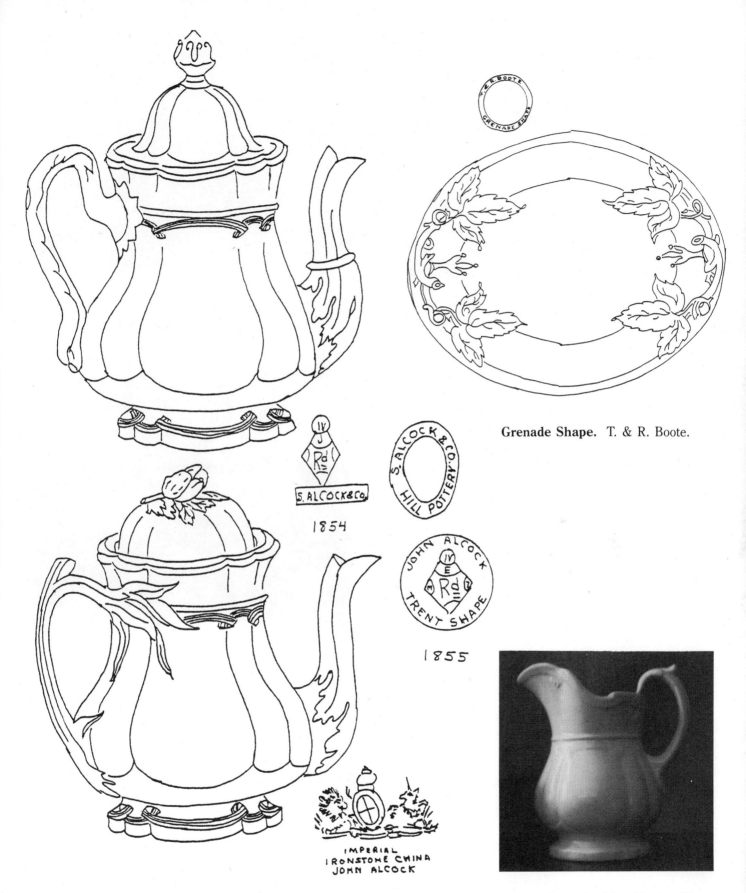

Grenade Shape. T. & R. Boote.

1854

1855

IMPERIAL
IRONSTONE CHINA
JOHN ALCOCK

Trent Shape. Samuel Alcock, registered 1854, and John Alcock, registered 1855. These two companies obviously used the same body shape for their teapots but added different handles and covers. Note the slight change in the spout.

Trent creamer by John Alcock. Photograph: Blair.

IMPERIAL
IRONSTONE
CHINA
JOHN ALCOCK

Paris Shape. John Alcock, registered 1857. The finial and accompanying foliage are the same as those on the oval **President Shape.** A sugar bowl has the same decor as **Chinese.**

*Very different is this ring handled **Paris Shape** gravy boat by John Alcock. Photograph: Dollard.*

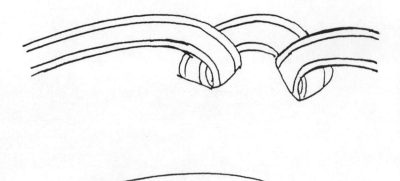

Stafford Shape. John Alcock. This is the same border as found on **Trent Shape.**

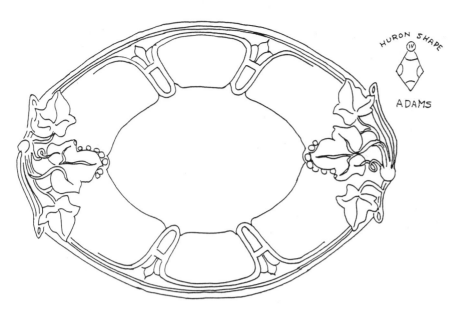

Huron *creamer by Adams, registered 1858. Photograph: Blair.*

Huron Shape. Adams, registered 1858.

*Large, low stew tureen in **Huron Shape** by Adams. Photograph: Blair.*

Haveloch Shape. Holland & Green used a ring handle, wheat border, with berries on the cover.

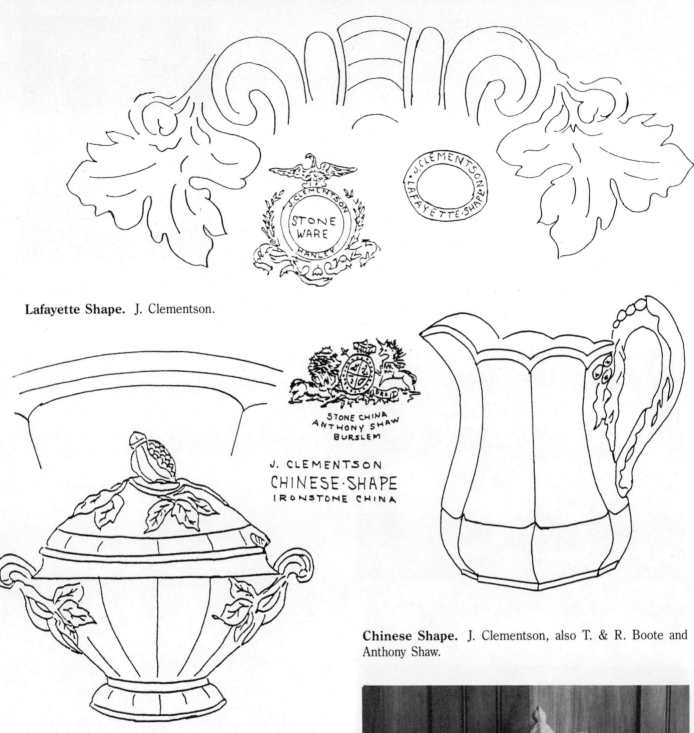

Lafayette Shape. J. Clementson.

STONE CHINA
ANTHONY SHAW
BURSLEM

J. CLEMENTSON
CHINESE·SHAPE
IRONSTONE CHINA

Chinese Shape. J. Clementson, also T. & R. Boote and Anthony Shaw.

***Chinese Shape** by T. & R. Boote. Pieces located by Tom Needham, Kansas. Photograph: Blair.*

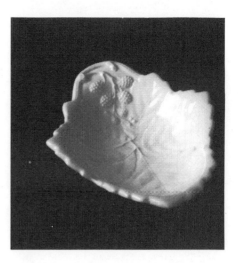

*Interesting detailed **Potomac Shape** relish dish by W. Baker & Co. Photograph: Dollard.*

*In the same flowing lines and with the same leaves and berries on cover and handles, Shaw superimposes the Sydenham leaf over the panels. We therefore nickname it **Chinese Sydenham.** Photograph: Groff.*

Potomac Shape (called **Blackberry**). W. Baker & Co., registered 1862.

Napier Shape. Bridgwood and Son. Ornate sugar bowl, 8½ " tall.

Union Shape. T. &. R. Boote, 9¾ " high, registered 1856.

Union Shape pitcher by T. &. R. Boote. Collection of Mr. and Mrs. William Horner. Photograph: Dr. Horner.

Citron Shape. J. Clementson, registered 1863. Detail of foliage at end of tray for sauce tureen. To the left is a top view of the tureen handle.

John Edwards of Fenton made this **St. Louis** *sugar bowl and chamber cover with well-potted finial, c. late 1850s. Photograph: Groff.*

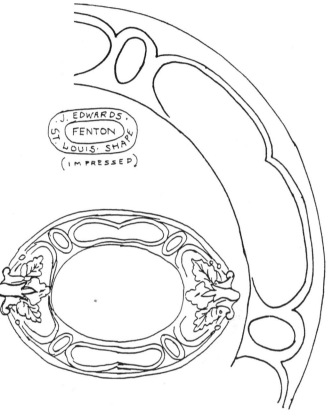

St. Louis Shape. John Edwards.

St. Louis finial. Side view.

*Vegetable bowl with trumpet flower finial in **Mobile Shape** by G. Bowers, beside a **Boote's 1851 Octagon** punch cup. Photograph: Blair.*

De Soto Shape. Thos. Hughes, registered 1855.

Sevres Shape. J. Clementson, John Edwards

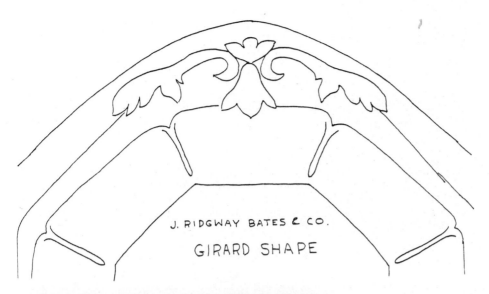

Girard Shape. J. Ridgway Bates.

Girard Shape milk jug by J. Ridgway Bates & Co. *Photograph: Blair.*

Asia Shape finial. G. Wooliscroft.

New York Shape shaving mug and horizontal toothbrush holder from a toilet set by J. Clementson. *Photograph: Blair.*

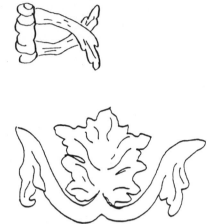

New York Shape. J. Clementson, registered 1858. To the right, above, are details of the handles and plate designs.

Two patterns that often are confused.
Left: **New York Shape.** Right:
Asia Shape.

*A wonderful find is this **New York Shape** chocolate pot located by the Blacks. Photograph: Black.*

New York Shape tea set main pieces.
Photograph: Blair.

Portland Shape. Elsmore & Forster.

Portland Shape by Elsmore & Forster. The remarkable bell-flower finials are a fascination to collectors. Collection of James and Doris Walker, New York. Photograph: Blair.

Classic Shape. T. &. R. Boote, 1868.

Syllabub bowl by T. &. R. Boote, 10" diameter, 3½ quart size, with the words, "Royal Patent," included in the mark. **Sydenham** *ladle,* **Scalloped Decagon** *syllabub cup. Collection of Mr. and Mrs. John Black. Photograph: Black.*

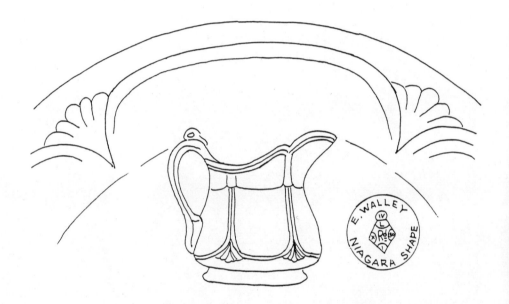

Niagara Shape. Edward Walley, registered 1856.

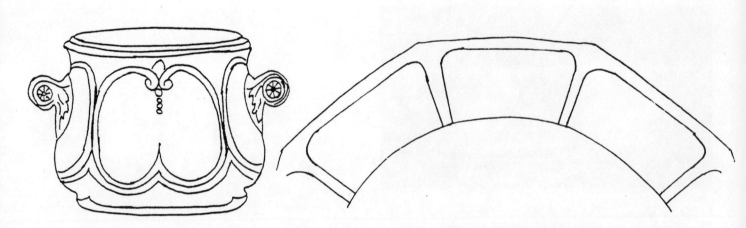

Virginia Shape. Brougham & Mayer, registered 1855.

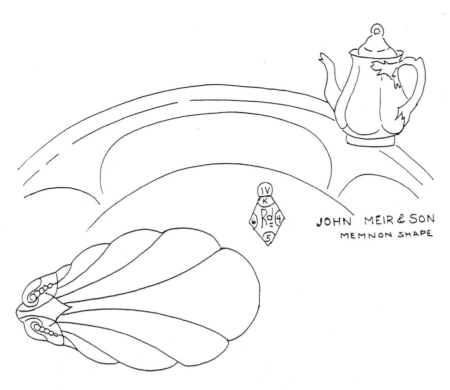

Memnon Shape. John Meir & Son, registered 1857.

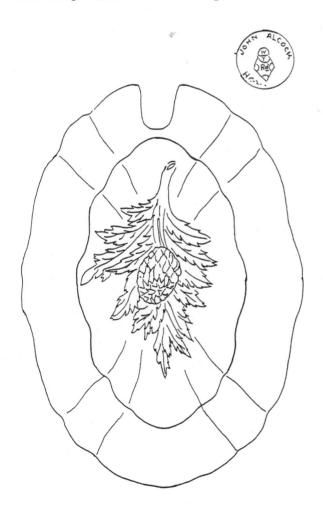

Baltimore Shape coffeepot by Brougham and Mayer, potted in the early 1850s. Owned by the Deimers in Delaware. Photograph: Deimer.

Hebe Shape. John Alcock, registered 1853.

9   Harvest Themes

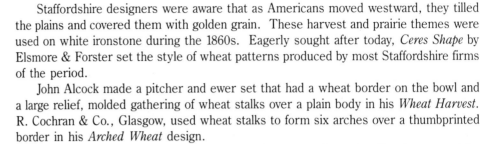

Staffordshire designers were aware that as Americans moved westward, they tilled the plains and covered them with golden grain. These harvest and prairie themes were used on white ironstone during the 1860s. Eagerly sought after today, *Ceres Shape* by Elsmore & Forster set the style of wheat patterns produced by most Staffordshire firms of the period.

John Alcock made a pitcher and ewer set that had a wheat border on the bowl and a large relief, molded gathering of wheat stalks over a plain body in his *Wheat Harvest*. R. Cochran & Co., Glasgow, used wheat stalks to form six arches over a thumbprinted border in his *Arched Wheat* design.

The common wheat motif has been reproduced continuously. By the turn of the century, the designs were vague, and the color was a creamy white rather than the blue-white employed by the early Staffordshire potteries. Today, several companies in England and the United States reproduce this white ironstone design.

The reproductions that confuse dealers and collectors alike are the excellent ones by R C (Red Cliff China), potted near Chicago in the mid-twentieth century. Pieces are always clearly marked, and sometimes impressed. W. Adams also made a creamy white wheat service that was as clearly detailed as the antique ironstone. It is clearly stamped *Made in England*—a twentieth-century marking.

The "most wanted" wheat pattern was named *Ceres* in honor of the Roman goddess of agriculture. This shape was registered by Elsmore & Forster, Tunstall in 1859, and continued in production later by Turner, Goddard & Co. A detail of the motif shows three rows of wheat grains in each head among graceful leaf stalks and includes a twisted rope band circling the bases and the necks.

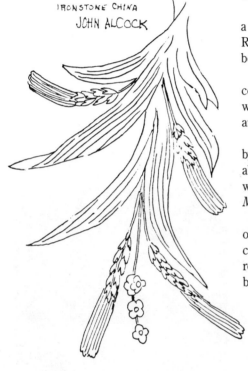

Ceres Shape *by Elsmore & Forster has been the best known white ironstone pattern through the years. Oval tureen, 16½", complete with cracker tray and ladle. Owners are Mr. and Mrs. John Black. Photograph: Black.*

Ceres toilet pieces by Elsmore & Forster, registered in 1859. The 1860s seemed to be the "wheat" years. Photograph: W. Wetherbee.

*This low, detailed **Ceres** compote by Elsmore & Forster was usually complemented by a set of shallow saucedishes. Treasured by Jane Diemer. Photograph: Diemer.*

*Covered **Ceres** hot toddy bowl registered in 1859 by Elsmore & Forster. Bowls like this usually came equipped with a ladle and a set of footed cups, Armbruster collection. Photograph: Armbruster.*

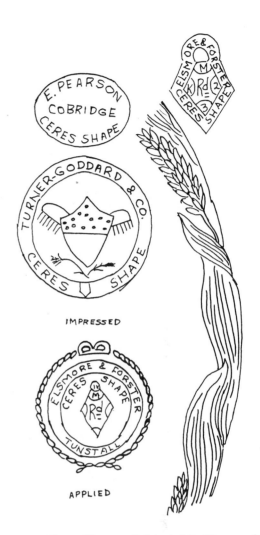

IMPRESSED

APPLIED

Ceres Shape. Originated by Elsmore & Forster in 1859, subsequently produced by Turner, Goddard & Co. and E. Pearson.

Basic family **Ceres** *circle. The creamer did not survive as well as other pieces. Photograph: Blair.*

Collectors have been especially fascinated by the *Corn and Oats* pattern, which is particularly adapted to the round and oval shapes. The grains are deeply impressed, and most pieces are bordered.

Corn and Oats. Davenport, also J. Wedgwood, registered 1863.

Corn and Oats, *a favorite pattern, potted by both J. Wedgwood and Davenport. Pitcher is owned by Jean Hogg, New York, and the other pieces by the Wetherbees. Photograph: Blair.*

Other more common table services in the *Wheat* pattern have twelve vertical melon-shaped ribs on the bowls and pitchers and a scalloped border deep inside the flatware. This most common *Wheat* form is topped with finials in the shape of an open sheaf resting on wheat heads and foliage. Among the manufacturers were Turner, Goddard & Co., Turner & Tomkinson, Elsmore & Forster, J. & G. Meakin, Wilkinson, W. & E. Corn, Hollinshead & Kirkham, and Baker & Co. No rope (cable) is included.

Wheat. Hollinshead & Kirkham, late J. Wedgwood, potted after 1876.

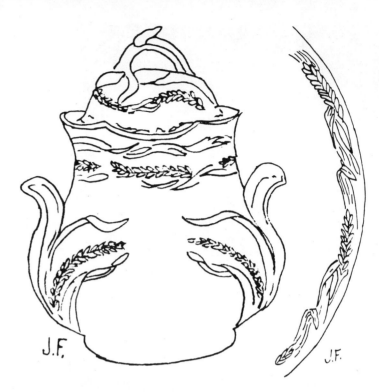

J.F.'s Wheat. No melon ribs are included with this 1860s pattern.

An example nicknamed *Wheat and Poppy* is also stamped *Prairie Shape*. This wheat pattern does not make use of the usual melon-shaped ribs or the wheat border. It often can be confused with a similar pattern nicknamed *Prairie Flowers*. The "wheat" heads in this second decoration have long beards. The field grasses, clover, and flowers impressed on these dishes are clear, sharp, and very detailed. The *Prairie Shape* was potted by both Livesley Powell and Joseph Clementson, registered in 1862, while *Prairie Flowers* was introduced by such experts as Livesley & Powell in 1862, and their successors, Powell & Bishop, circa 1876. *Scotia Shape* from the kilns of F. Jones & Co., Longton, circa 1870, is bordered with wheat and poppies and has convex ribs.

Prairie Flowers. Livesley Powell, Powell & Bishop.

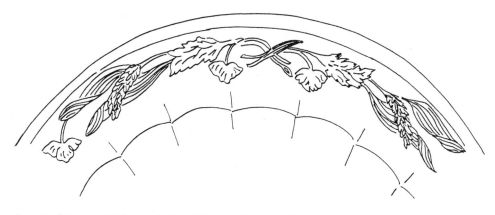

Scotia Shape. F. Jones & Co. **Poppy Shape.** No potter included.

Scotia Shape sharply detailed round soap dish. Liner is not perforated as in butter dishes. By F. Jones & Co. Photograph: W. Wetherbee.

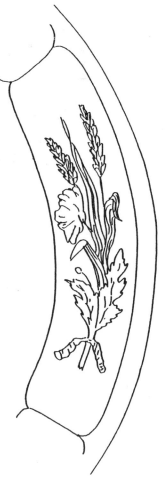

Prairie Shape. J. Clementson, registered 1862.

A design marked *Pearl* has been often called *Wheat and Clover*. The decorations are related to other wheat patterns but are elaborated by a ribbon bow and clover leaves with blossoms amid the usual wheat.

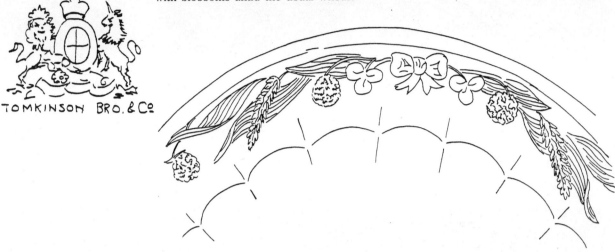

Wheat and Clover. Tomkinson Bros. & Co., Turner & Tomkinson. Ford Challinor & Co., and Taylor Brothers.

Wheat and Clover teapot and larger coffeepot collected by Mr. and Mrs. Gary Grove, Pennsylvania.

Wheat and Blackberry. J. & G. Meakin, J. F., E. Pearson, W. Taylor, Robert Cochran & Co., and also an American pottery company, St. Johns Chinaware Co. in Canada. The relief molding looks almost carved.

Wheat and Blackberry *ewer and basin by J. & G. Meakin,*
with deeply sculptured berries and leaves. Owned by Warren and
Cristie Wetherbee. Photograph: Blair.

Wheat in the Meadow. Powell
& Bishop registered 1869.

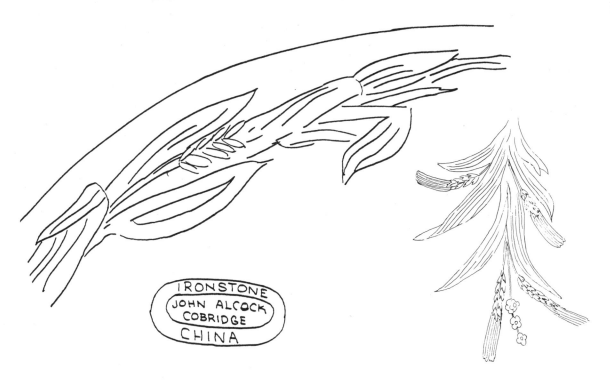

Wheat Harvest. John Alcock covered both sides of a plain
pitcher.

Arched Wheat. R. Cochran & Co., Glasgow.

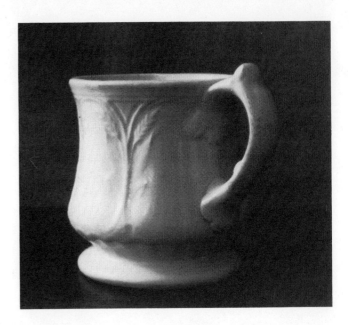

Collectible toilet set mug in **Arched Wheat** *by Cochran. Photograph: Groff.*

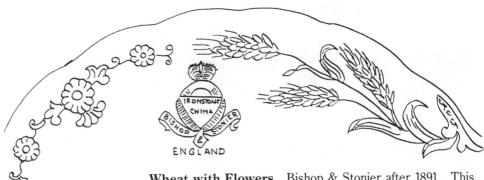

Wheat with Flowers. Bishop & Stonier after 1891. This is one of the later wheat patterns. It's repeated three times around a soup plate border.

Wheat and Grape. Unmarked. This decor, a cluster of grapes with leaves, was copied from a wheat-bordered compote.

Roped Wheat. Furnival & Sons, England. This after-1891 pattern is sharply detailed—unusual in the late-nineteenth-century sets.

Wheat and ribs with a different treatment. **Four-Square Wheat** *by the Scottish potter Cochran. Probably late nineteenth century. Photograph: Blair.*

Canada has been attributed to Meikle Bros., Liverpool. Shown are two marks found on soup tureens in this pattern.

Canada *wheat and poppy design registered in 1877. No potter's mark on soup tureen. Owned by James and Doris Walker, New York. Photograph: Blair.*

Nearly all the bread platters (which were mostly American made) had some sort of wheat motif. The one shown here, however, has been attributed to Davenport, who admonished, "Where reason rules, the appetite obeys." This server has also been seen in the bright colors of majolica with the same decor and slogan.

The word "ironstone" often brings to mind that most famous decor of old white china, a wheat design. This fact was driven home most forcibly by Norman Rockwell, the great American illustrator. He chose a scene called "Freedom from Want" for use in one of his Four Freedom series. It pictures a middle-class American family gathered happily and hungrily around the laden table set with plain ironstone on spotless linen. Grandpa hovers over Grandma as she proudly bears the crispy, brown turkey on the traditional enormous ironstone platter. In the foreground shines a large, covered, blue-white ironstone tureen with melon shaped ribs and borders of heavily embossed wheat heads and stalks. This well-publicized wheat pattern has grown to symbolize the fruitfulness of our farms.

10   Leaves That Decorate

*I went down into the garden of nuts
to see the fruits of the valley,
and to see whether the vine flourished
and the pomegranates budded.*
—Song of Solomon

Wheat, holly and berries, and oak leaves with acorns were echoes from the decorations on the earlier painted porcelains and also from some of the Staffordshire blue borders.

When the use of transfer-decorated services yielded to white ironstone, potters had to be more exact in the molding of the finials, which were shaped like nuts, fruits, gourds, cones, and acorns. The transfers could mask poorer constructions, but potters of white ironstone had to become adept at forming realistic sculptured handles and finials. Details in leaves and vines also became more precise, as buyers were attracted by the clear-cut decorations.

The shapes covered with leaves and vines were seldom named or dated by the makers. However, the majority of them boasted a potter's mark. And by researching the years that the potteries existed and noticing the few dates stamped on pieces, we conclude that most of these foliage patterns were made in the 1860s. Exceptions are *Ivy 1857* and *Hanging Arch 1858*.

Leaves of grape, oak, ivy, holly, apple, and berry were often wrapped around the bodies under finials, handles, and spouts. Blackberries, other berries, and grapes peeked out of their leaves much as they do in our gardens today.

In this way, alert potters appealed to the love of husbandry evidenced by the westward-moving American families.

*Treasured **Fig** pieces by Davenport. Punch or toddy cups are usually not marked by potters. Photograph: Blair.*

Fig. J. Wedgwood, also Davenport, registered 1856.

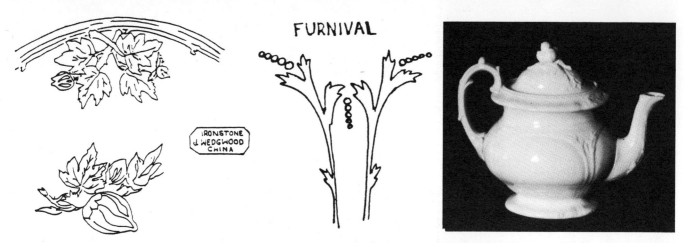

FURNIVAL

IRONSTONE
J. WEDGWOOD
CHINA

*This early Furnival teapot differs from other pieces of the 1850s because of the low, oval shape. The finial is made up of a **Berry Cluster.** Photograph: Groff.*

*Both Davenport and J. Wedgwood potted this **Fig Cousin.** The same foliage and small fruit decorate the round bodies. Collection of Ray and Priscilla Casavant. Photograph: Groff.*

STONE CHINA
JOHN MEIR & SON
TUNSTALL
WARRANTED

Nut with Bud. John Meir & Son. Notice the same nut finial on **Leaf Fan** by Bridgwood & Clarke.

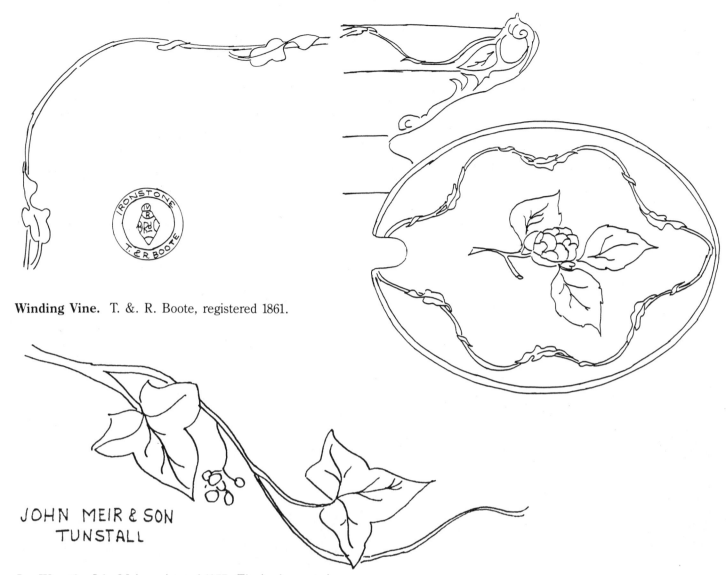

Winding Vine. T. &. R. Boote, registered 1861.

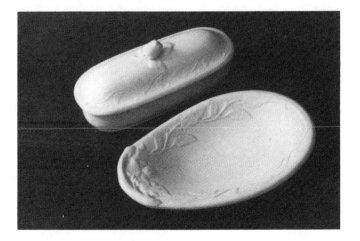

JOHN MEIR & SON
TUNSTALL

Ivy Wreath. John Meir, registered 1857. The ivy leaves twine around the edge of tureen covers. The lower part of the body of water pitchers is circled by a wide band of these leaves. The neck is also wreathed.

Wreath of Leaves wind around the edges of this brush holder and relish dish. There is an ironstone stamp on each, but the potter's name is not included. Photograph: Dollard.

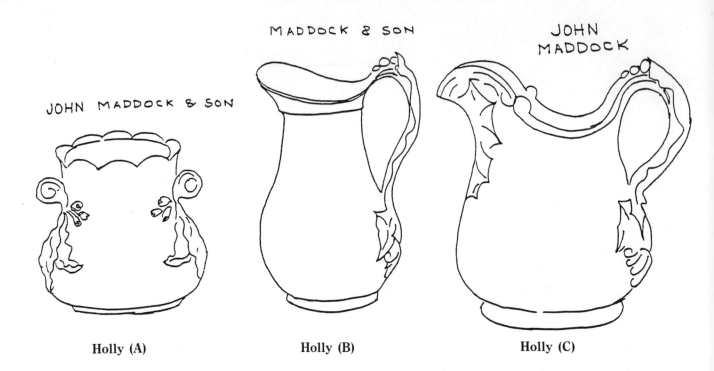

JOHN MADDOCK & SON

MADDOCK & SON

JOHN MADDOCK

Holly (A)

Holly (B)

Holly (C)

Holly. Maddock (& Son). Here are three variations of this pattern. All employ holly berries and the same leaf wrapped around the handles of the pitchers. Notice similar decor on **Grenade Shape** and **Chinese Shape** pitchers. **Chinese Shape** also portrays the body decoration used on **Holly (A)**.

Holly pitchers in three sizes by Maddock. From the collections of three New York families: the Pecoras, the Hoggs, and the Wetherbees. Photograph: Blair.

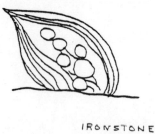

IRONSTONE
CHINA
E. & C. CHALLINOR

Winterberry. Edward Clarke.

Winterberry *pattern toothbrush holder with ventilating hole, Edward Clark. Photograph: Blair.*

Loop and Dot. E. & C. Challinor after 1862.

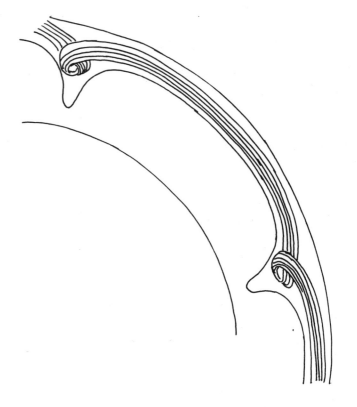

Pomegranate *by J. F. uses the same finial and foliage as Clementson's* **Columbia Shape** *and Boote's* **Chinese.** *Borders are the same as* **Trent Shape.** *Collection of James and Doris Walker, New York. Photograph: Blair.*

Acorn. Unmarked.

This pair of Wedgwood & Co. jugs has been nicknamed "Poison Ivy" but we rechristened it a **Branch of Three Leaves.** *Photograph: W. Wetherbee.*

One-cup teapot.

Branch of Three Leaves. Wedgwood & Co. This pattern has great detail and is seldom found crazed or stained.

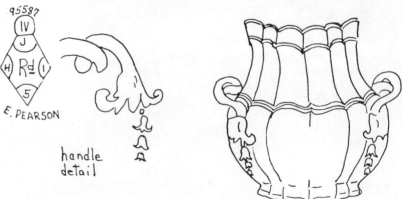

Dangling Tulip. E. Pearson, registered 1854.

White Oak and Acorn. Holland & Green. This pattern was named, but the letters were blurred on this beautiful pitcher.

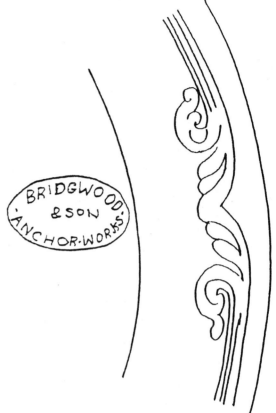

Scrolled Boarder. Bridgwood & Son.

Tiny Oak and Acorn. J. W. Pankhurst. The oval tureen measures 12″ long.

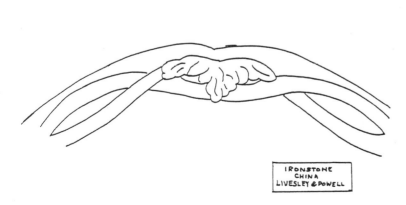

Leaf and Crossed Ribbon. Livesley & Powell

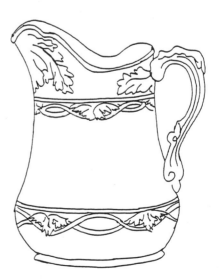

Cookie plates are hard to unearth. This one is **Leaf and Crossed Ribbon** *by Livesley & Powell. Photograph: Blair.*

Panelled Scroll. Rectangular mark illegible.

ROYAL STONE CHINA
WEDGWOOD & CO.

STONE GRANITE
(impressed)

Arbor Vine. Wedgwood & Co.

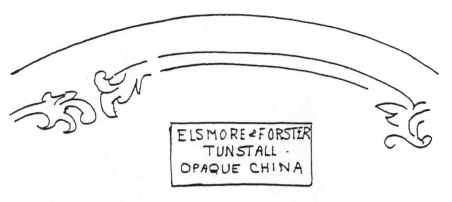

Little Scroll. Elsmore & Forster. This pattern includes a large oval sugar bowl with a rosebud finial. Perhaps this body in both round and oval shapes is best known for its two-color blue over-decorations, and for its cobalt blue and copper band treatment.

Little Scroll round teapot by Elsmore & Forster. Photograph: Groff.

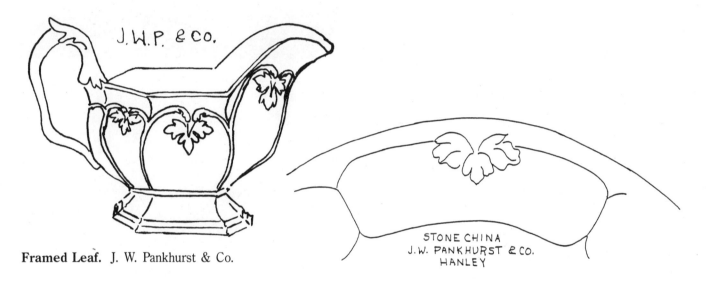

Framed Leaf. J. W. Pankhurst & Co.

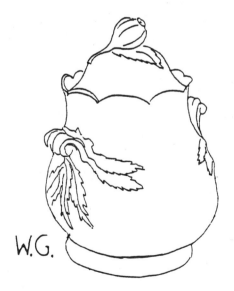

Gooseberry. Marked W. G. (?). These letters may have referred to "white granite."

This teapot boasts a pear finial over curved vertical panels. By J. Alcock. Photograph: Dollard.

This gleaming **Starred Leaf** *pitcher was potted by T. &. R. Boote. From Armbruster collection. Photograph: Blair.*

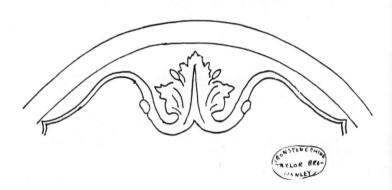

Leaf Focus. Taylor Bros. This pattern is similar to **New York Shape.**

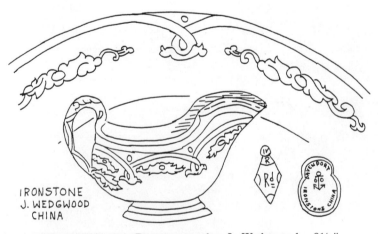

Sharon Arch. Davenport, also J. Wedgwood. 9½" soup bowl, registered 1861. Gravy boat, unmarked.

Sharon Arch *patterned dishes potted by both Davenport and J. Wedgwood are unusually heavy. Dinner plate weighs two pounds; ring-handled pitcher, four pounds; covered vegetable dish, three pounds. Handleless cup is pictured, but handled version was also made. Photograph: Blair.*

Leaf Fan *made by Bridgwood & Clarke has a fan of leaves under the handle. Photograph: Blair.*

This **Medallion Scroll** *tureen is by Clementson Bros. Photograph: Groff. Also see photograph, page 155.*

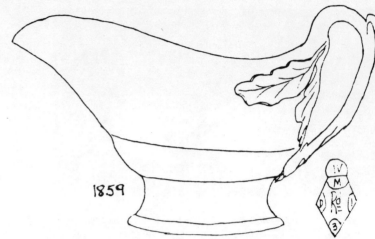

1859

Draped Leaf (A). James Edwards & Son.

EDWARDS

Draped Leaf (B). James Edwards.

Draped Leaf (C). Bridgwood & Clarke. Heavy bodied, three-quart pitcher.

Draped Leaf (D). Henry Alcock & Co.

Gourd. James Edwards & Son.

*Small **Hanging Arch** pitcher by James Edwards & Son is from the collection of James and Michelle Sempere. Photograph: Blair.*

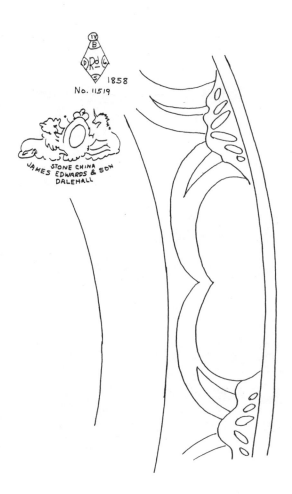

Hanging Arch. James Edwards & Son. Platter is 16½ " long.

Hanging Arch *pattern includes twig handles and finial with surrounding fruit and leaves. By James Edwards & Son. Collection of James and Doris Walker. Photograph: Blair.*

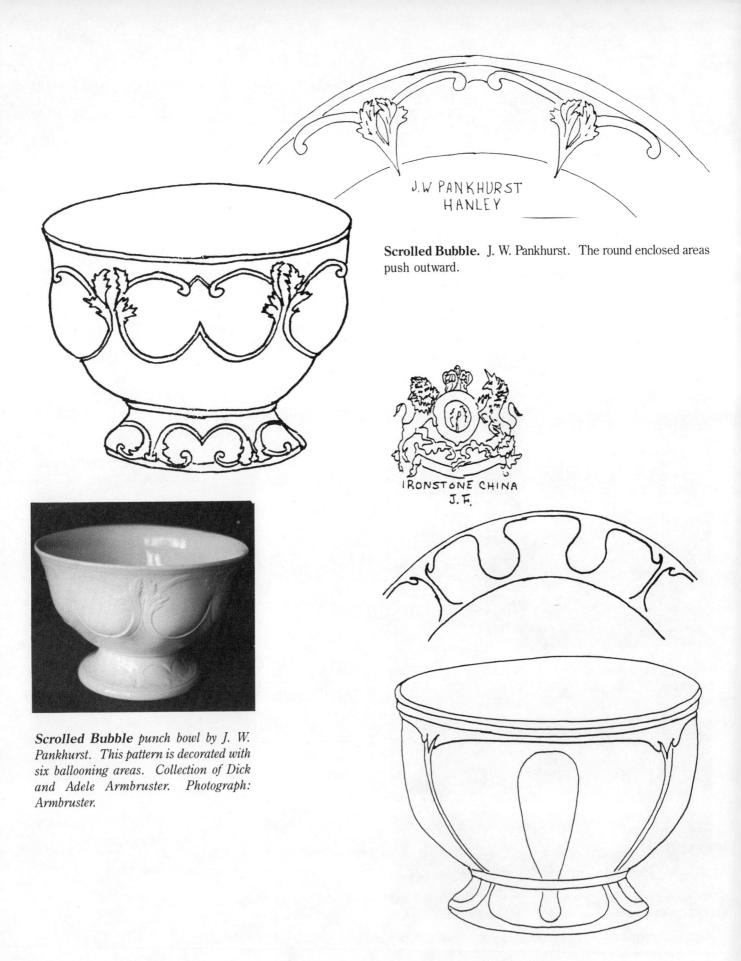

J.W. PANKHURST
HANLEY

Scrolled Bubble. J. W. Pankhurst. The round enclosed areas push outward.

IRONSTONE CHINA
J. F.

Scrolled Bubble *punch bowl by J. W. Pankhurst. This pattern is decorated with six ballooning areas. Collection of Dick and Adele Armbruster. Photograph: Armbruster.*

Loop and Line. Marked J. F.

Fleur-de-Lis with Leaf. J. W. Pankhurst.

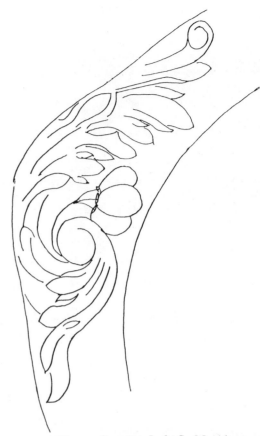

Cherry Scroll. J. & G. Meakin.

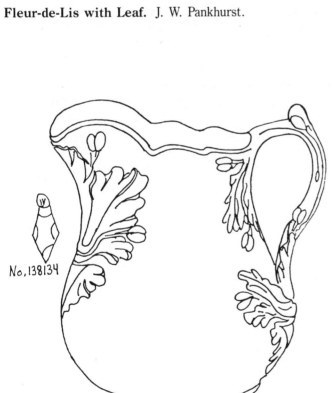

Draped Leaf with Berries. No potter named. Early numbering system.

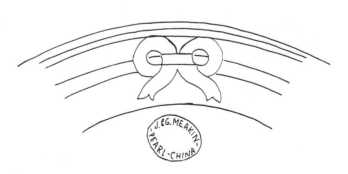

Bow Knot. J. & G. Meakin.

Plain Berlin *sugar bowl. Liddle, Elliott & Son. A plain pattern (except for the nut finial) created before plain patterns came into style.*

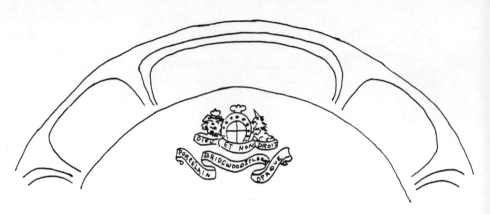

Alternate Loops. Bridgwood & Clarke, who potted from 1857-1864.

11   Flowers To Lift the Heart

And each flower and herb on Earth's dark breast
Rose from the dream of its wintry rest.

—Shelley

After 1860, few panelled jugs and octagonal tureens were made. Most bodies were round, pear-shaped surfaces decorated with low-relief moldings of naturalistic leaves and flowers.

Earlier in the 1840s, rosebud finials topped the *Gothic Rose* and the squared *Rosebud*. In the 1850s *Chinese* and *Trent Shapes* were topped with rosebuds, and *Prize Bloom* looked like an open wild rose. In the 1860s, there were several wild rose decorations and the popular *Moss Rose*, which was true to life right down to the bristling stems.

Some patterns wind around the edges of plates and the bodies of pitchers in a deeply impressed wreath. Most preferable of these are *Morning Glory* with its trumpet flower, *Bordered Fuchsia* with its typical hanging blooms, and *Lily Shape* with its calla hidden between the leaves. We see the fuchsia again in the *Laurel* pattern and in the precise blooms of *Fuchsia*, potted by J. & G. Meakin and Jones.

The lily-of-the-valley drawings and pictures are grouped together. *Hyacinth*, potted by Wedgwood & Co., bears little resemblance to the American hyacinth that bursts up in our spring borders, but my flower catalog depicts it exactly and labels it "English Hyacinth." The motif looks like the several lily-of-the-valley patterns, and all are compatible in the same table setting. *Shaw's Lily-of-the-Valley* has little bells springing from both sides of the stem. Later, a copper band and tea leaf motif were added to this shape. *Western Shape* had a chain border, and J.F. added a border of thumbprints to these lily-of-the-valley designs. Wild poppies and clover are intermingled with grains in some of the wheat patterns and in *Meadow Bouquet*.

In the chapter describing unusual white ironstone, you'll find three patterns with flowers that completely cover the tea plates. These floral embellishments lifted many nineteenth-century hearts, just as flowers do today.

IRONSTONE
CHINA
J. & G. MEAKIN

Garden Sprig. J. & G. Meakin. Five motifs around plates.

Garden Sprig teapot in lines that were to be used in the 1870s and 1880s. Potter was J. & G. Meakin. Photograph: Dollard.

*No photograph can do justice to this **Morning Glory** pattern by Elsmore & Forster. Sharply detailed, the vines wind all over the bodies of serving pieces. Photograph: Blair.*

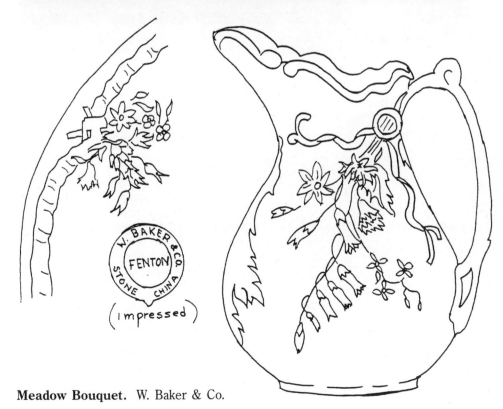

W. BAKER & CO.
FENTON
STONE CHINA

(impressed)

Meadow Bouquet. W. Baker & Co.

103

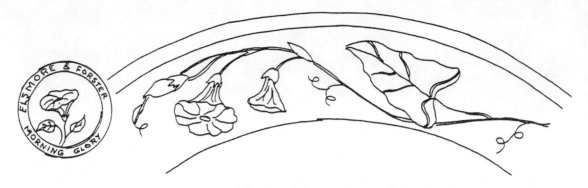

Morning Glory. Elsmore & Forster impressed mark on a raised pad.

Bordered Fuchsia. Anthony Shaw. Also see page 155.

Bordered Fuchsia *teapot by A. Shaw, no lid. Photograph: Blair.*

Flora. Wedgwood & Co. Covered dishes are decorated with flowers in medallions and topped with gooseberry finials.

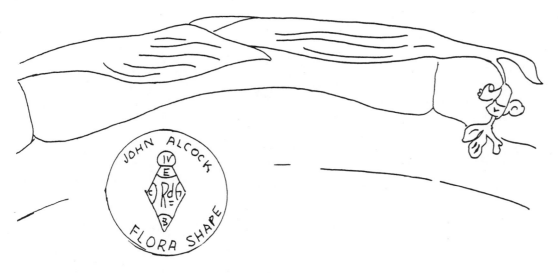

Flora Shape. John Alcock, registered 1855. Beverage servers are striking, with long vertical shards hanging down.

*John Alcock's **Flora Shape** includes ribs and draping spray on this sugar bowl. Owned by Jane Diemer. Photograph: Diemer.*

*A **Forget-Me-Not** type motif by Wood, Rathbone & Co. decorates this teapot. Owned by the Armbrusters. Photograph: Armbruster.*

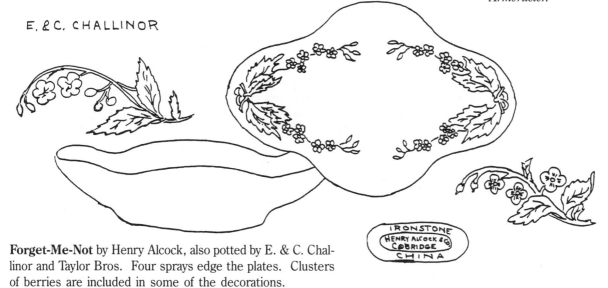

Forget-Me-Not by Henry Alcock, also potted by E. & C. Challinor and Taylor Bros. Four sprays edge the plates. Clusters of berries are included in some of the decorations.

Shaw's Spray. Anthony Shaw.

Bordered Gooseberry. This pattern always seems to be unmarked.

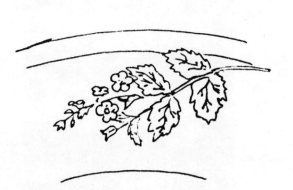

Wild Flower. No potter named.

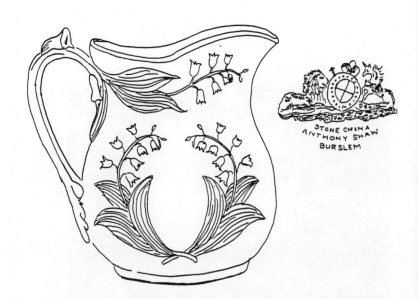

Shaw's Lily of the Valley. Anthony Shaw. Finial is a large, three-dimensional bellflower. This design has been found on bone dishes, which were not usual in a set of early white ironstone.

Shaw's Lily of the Valley. Bellflower finial, with small bellflowers in sides of stalk. Collection of Winfield and Lyn Wetherbee. Photograph: Blair.

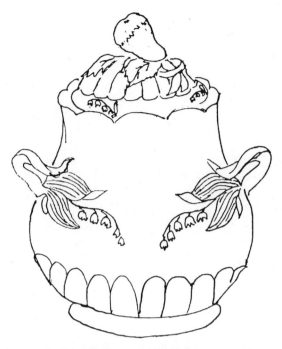

Lily of the Valley with thumbprints. J.F.

*James Edward's **Lily-of-the-Valley** gravy boat, registered in 1858. Photograph: Groff.*

Flowering Vine.

No. 13858⁵

Lily-of-the-Valley. James Edwards, registered 1858. The chowder cup is 3½″ wide and holds 16 oz.; saucer is 7″ in diameter.

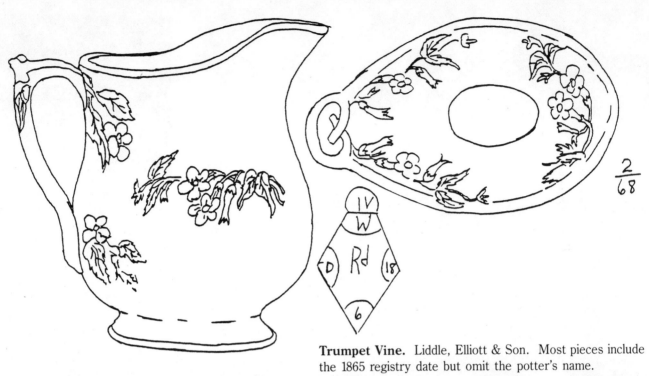

Trumpet Vine. Liddle, Elliott & Son. Most pieces include the 1865 registry date but omit the potter's name.

Hyacinth. Wedgwood & Co.

Bordered Hyacinth. W. Baker & Co.

DETAIL OF FLOWER

STONE CHINA
HOPE & CARTER
BURSLEM

Western Shape. Hope & Carter, W. & E. Corn, registered 1862.

Lily of the Valley motif is shown on **Western Shape** *sugar bowl by W. &. E. Corn and toddy cup by Anthony Shaw. Collection of James and Doris Walker. Photograph: Blair.*

J. & G. MEAKIN
IRONSTONE CHINA

Moss Rose. J. & G. Meakin. Motif detail on end of liner for soup tureen. Serving pieces are bulbous in shape. The teapot handle is forked at the top.

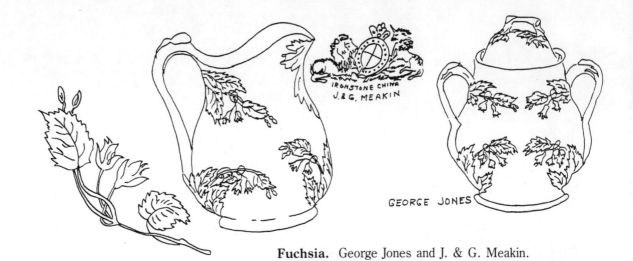

Fuchsia. George Jones and J. & G. Meakin.

Fuchsia vegetable server by J. & G. Meakin.   Photograph: Blair.

Laurel. Wedgwood & Co.

Laurel teapot liberally decorated by Wedgwood & Co. **Fuchsia** *handleless cup and saucer.   Collection of Mr. and Mrs. John Black, New York.   Photograph: Black.*

Nosegay. E. & C. Challinor. This dainty design is repeated five times.

Bellflower *waste bowl from a tea set and teapot by J. Edwards. Collection of James and Doris Walker, New York. Photograph: Blair.*

Bellflower. John Edwards.

Lily Shape, Corn.

Wild Rose Twig. C. Meigh & Son after 1860.

Mocho. T. & R. Boote, registered 1863. Some pieces have an unusual blue pad with name and registry. Nicknamed "Little Palm."

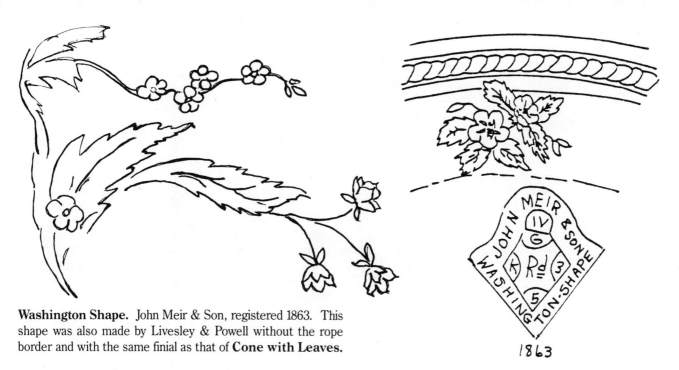

Washington Shape. John Meir & Son, registered 1863. This shape was also made by Livesley & Powell without the rope border and with the same finial as that of **Cone with Leaves.**

1863

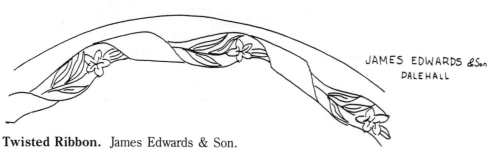

JAMES EDWARDS &Son
DALEHALL

Twisted Ribbon. James Edwards & Son.

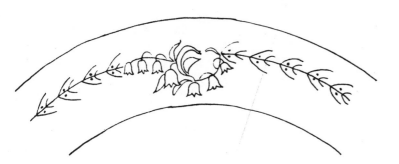

Bell Tracery. Holland & Green. Dainty design on lightweight ironstone.

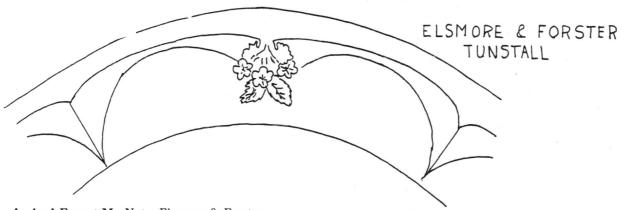

ELSMORE & FORSTER
TUNSTALL

Arched Forget-Me-Not. Elsmore & Forster.

Star Flower. J. W. Pankhurst. Foliage around the finial is different from the tiny leaves near the flowers.

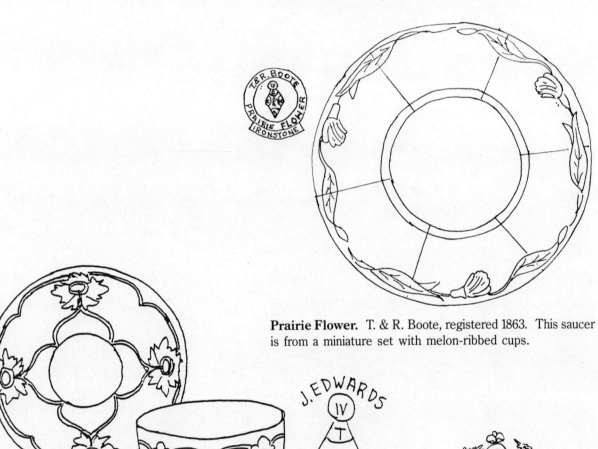

Prairie Flower. T. & R. Boote, registered 1863. This saucer is from a miniature set with melon-ribbed cups.

Tuscan Shape. James Edwards, registered 1867. Design copied later in porcelain.

12 Vintage Patterns

The graceful leaves of the trailing grapevine and the bountiful clusters it bears have appealed to man through the ages. Ancient civilizations often depicted vine and grape motifs.

These same decorations can be found pressed or etched in molded glass, cast in early silver, painted on antique English porcelains, interwoven in the wood borders of Staffordshire blues, and included in other early fruit basket china patterns.

The earliest white ironstone vintage design was probably used in the *Montpelier Shape* by John Ridgway & Co. The grapes and leaves continued until they were last seen on the fabled *Fox and Grapes* after 1891.

Man will continue to use the leaves for food and medicine, the fruit for nourishment, and the dormant vines for making baskets and wreaths. Grapes are an integral part of man's daily life.

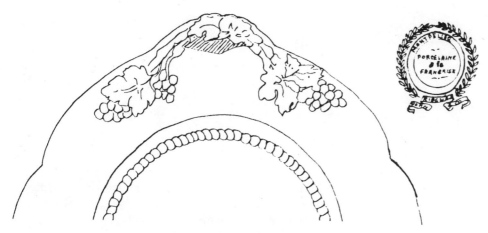

Montpelier Shape. John Ridgway & Co. Some serving pieces have an octagonal shape. This drawing is taken from a low doughnut stand.

J.F. designed this **Panelled Grape** *sugar bowl and large covered tureen. The little pieces from the "salesman's sample" are unmarked. Photograph: W. Wetherbee.*

Mark found on a **Grape Octagon** pitcher potted between 1853 and 1855.

E. CHALLINOR
& CO.

Grape Octagon. E. Challinor & Co., J. Clementson, Brougham & Mayer, Livesley Powell, Thomas Walker, Hulme & Booth, Venables Mann & Co., J.F. and Hulme & Booth registered this shape in 1848. Two others registered it in 1851. Different potters varied the placement of the grapes. A cluster of grapes often served as the finial.

Grape Octagon miniature tea set potted by Clementson displayed beside standard teapot in Boote's 1851 Octagon Shape with ringed handle. From the collection of Mr. and Mrs. James Walker. Photograph: Blair.

Grape Octagon *gravy boat.   Unmarked.   Photograph: Groff.*

Grape Octagon *sugar bowl by E. Challinor & Co.   Some finials were grapes, and others had a crabstock handle.   Photograph: Blair.*

Panelled Grape.   Marked J. F.   Also used by Edward Pearson.

Vintage Shape named by Adams, later repeated more extensively by E. & C. Challinor, circa 1865.   It has been nicknamed **Grape and Medallion.**

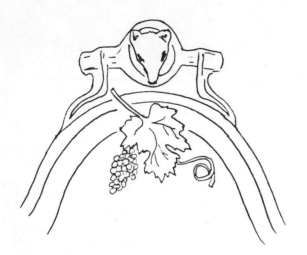

Fox and Grapes. Thomas Furnival & Sons, potted after 1891.

Collectors love mugs! Displayed are a shaving mug in **Fuchsia** *shape by J. & G. Meakin and a cider mug in* **Vintage Shape** *by E. & C. Challinor. Photograph: Groff.*

Grape Clusters. Davenport.

Grape Clusters *chamber pot made by Davenport in 1869 and* **Grape Cluster with Chain** *large jug. Two closely related, vintage patterns. Photograph: Blair.*

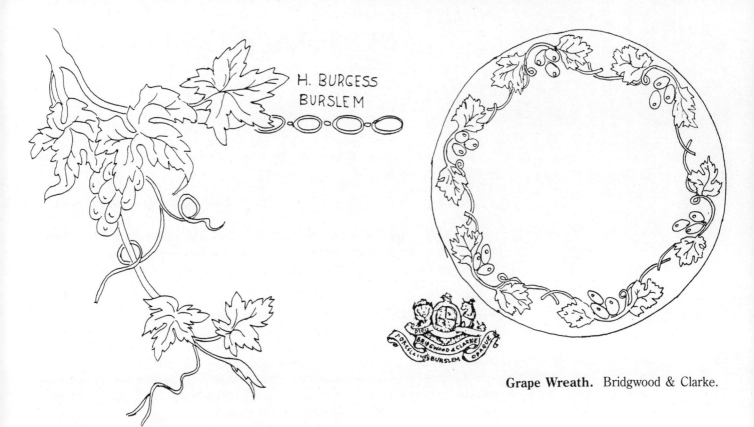

H. BURGESS
BURSLEM

Grape Wreath. Bridgwood & Clarke.

Grape Cluster with Chain. Henry Burgess. Motif taken from the side of a large milk jug.

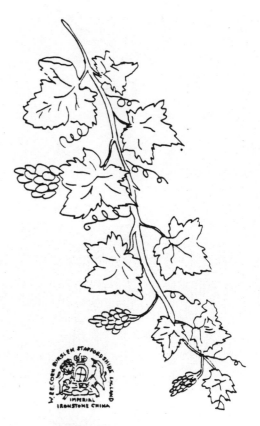

Ribbed Grape. W. & E. Corn. This long vine travels vertically.

Vintage Beauty syrup pitcher. *Uncommon, no lid. Potted well, with its vine over the ribs. J.F. Photograph: Blair.*

13   Ribbed Decors

Shortly after Elsmore & Forster created their noteworthy *1859 Ceres Shape,* other potters used the fashionable ribs, too. Many adapted the *Ceres* melon ribs to other wheat patterns, such as *Scotia, Wheat and Clover,* and *Wheat.* Some impressed other decorations in relief, such as *Vintage Beauty* by J.F. and the later *Ribbed Oak & Acorn* by Pankhurst.

Ribbed Bud and *Full Ribbed* pieces, both by J. W. Pankhurst, are much in demand by white ironstone devotees today. The *Ribbed Bud* butter dish is unusual, having been reported only once. The bowl and pitcher sets combine a graceful pitcher and a small ewer that opens like a flower. John Alcock's *Ribbed Berry* blends well with these two patterns.

The borders of plates and bodies of the serving tureens and jugs are completely covered with small ribs, foliage, and vines in these three shapes: J. & G. Meakin's *Ribbed Raspberry with Bloom, Ribbed Chain* by J. W. Pankhurst, and Adam's 1862 *Dover Shape.* These three patterns work well together in the same table settings.

Ribs were evidenced during the last quarter of the 1800s, as lady-finger ribs covered the outside of round and square nested open bowls. Soon, however, the ceramics designers put aside the ribbed embellishments for other pursuits.

Ribbed Bud sauce tureen by Pankhurst. Buds on the finial, under the handle, and on the ends of the tray are checked. Collection of John and Jane Yunginger, Minnesota. Photograph: Blair.

Ribbed Bud. J. W. Pankhurst. Unusual footed butter dish.

Three-piece box soap dish in **Ribbed Bud** *by Pankhurst. Photograph: Blair.*

Unusual butter dish in **Full Ribbed** *by Pankhurst. The bottom, which does not show in photograph, is a shallow dish (no foot). Photograph: W. Wetherbee.*

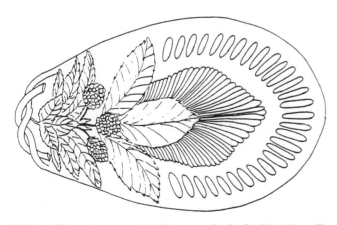

Ribbed Raspberry with Bloom. J. & G. Meakin. The bodies of all servers were covered with design. Tureens included the blossoms as well as the berries, leaves, ribs, and grooves.

Full Ribbed. J. W. Pankhurst.

Full-Ribbed Shape *fashioned as a ewer with flowerlike bowl, manufactured by J. W. Pankhurst. Collected by the Diemers in Delaware. Photograph: Diemer.*

Ribbed Raspberry with Bloom *by J. & G. Meakin is a pattern that covers most of the bodies of serving dishes and the complete borders of plates. Blooms are seen on covers. Collection of John Black. Photograph: Black.*

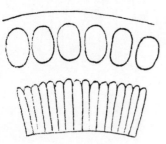

Major pieces of tea set in **Ribbed Raspberry with Bloom** *by J. & G. Meakin. Photograph: Blair.*

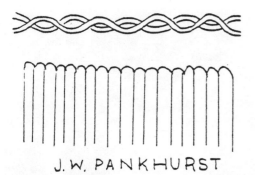

Ribbed Chain. J. W. Pankhurst. Covered serving dishes were fully decorated with chain, ribs, and foliage, and used twisted twig handles.

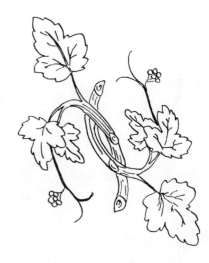

Many fine ribs cover the edges of plates and bodies of tureens in this **Ribbed Chain** *by J. W. Pankhurst. Photograph: Groff.*

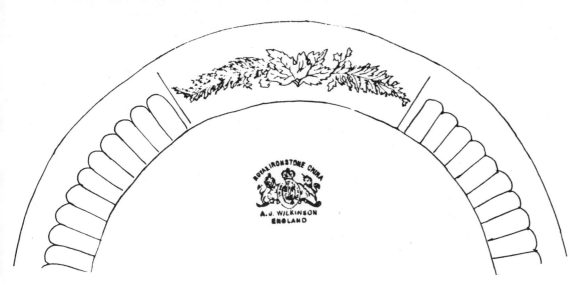

Ribbed Fern. A. J. Wilkinson, after 1891. These ribs are convex.

Ribbed Berry pitcher by John Alcock showing decoration super-imposed on ribs. Owned by James and Doris Walker, New York. Photograph: Blair.

Jug in **Empress Shape** *by W. Adams. Beware of "repros" in this pattern. Photograph: Black.*

Ribbed Berry. John Alcock. Detail of leaves with berries molded over the narrow ribs of a pitcher.

Ribbed lady fingers covered sides of nested serving dishes, both round and square, during the last quarter of the nineteenth century.

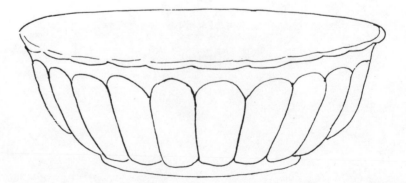

Dover Shape. W. Adams, registered 1862. Concave ribs on plates, convex on servers.

14   Old Pattern Revival

Many of the English potters who made porcelains, Parian, and bone china decorated their wares with themes from Greek and Roman mythology. Borders were often classic, echoing the patterns used in the architecture from these earlier periods.

Athens Shape was first made by Podmore & Walker and was registered in 1842—the earliest marked date I have seen on white ironstone. Most pieces of this pattern were re-offered and marked by P. & W.'s successors, Wedgwood & Co., after 1860. Perhaps this shape was revived at the same time other potters returned to the familiar Greek and Roman lines.

Athenia, with its geometric band; *Athena Shape,* with a meander border; and *Athens Shape,* with an acanthus trim, have similar names and are clearly dated from the mid-1860s.

J. W. Pankhurst edged plates with a narrow *Greek Key,* and Elsmore & Forster did their usual excellent potting with a wider Greek key in their *Olympic Shape.*

Olympic themes featuring the laurel wreaths that honored Greek athletes were also used. *Laurel Wreath* was offered by Elsmore & Forster in 1867. The same shape has been found, marked *Victory Shape,* by the same potter. A year later, F. Jones & Co. marketed a leaf and ear of corn wreath decoration on the sides of beverage jugs and sugar bowls.

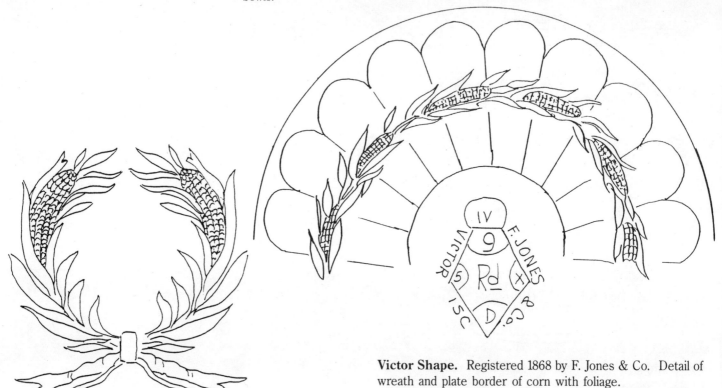

Victor Shape. Registered 1868 by F. Jones & Co. Detail of wreath and plate border of corn with foliage.

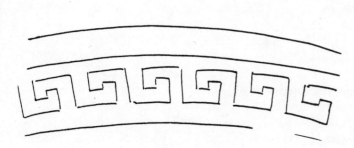

Greek Key. J. W. Pankhurst.

Victor Shape pitcher potted by F. Jones. Owned by John and Jane Yunginger, Minnesota. Photograph: Blair.

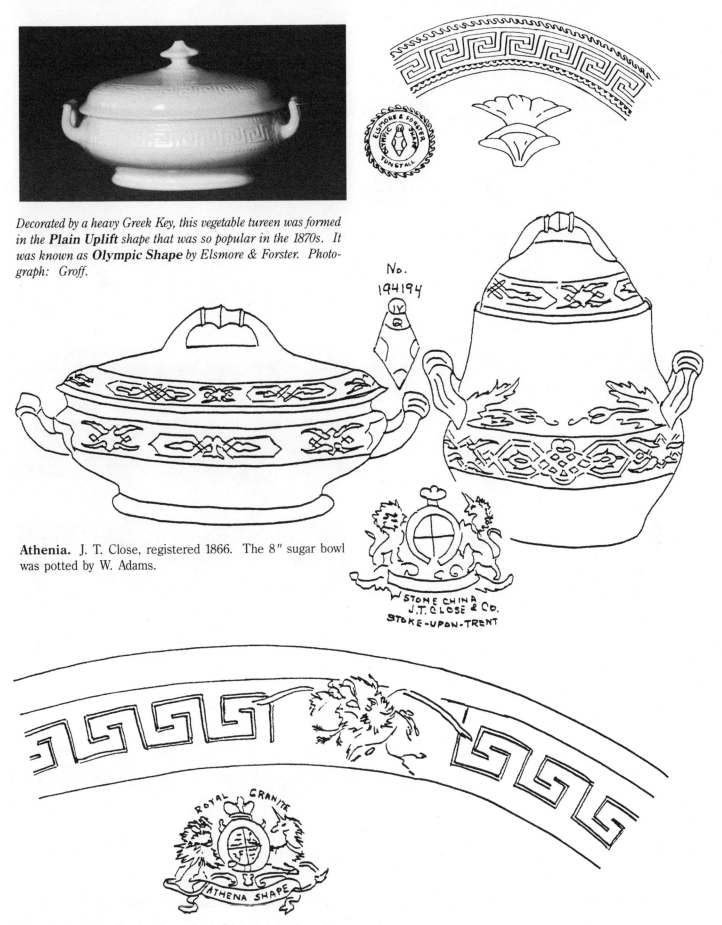

Decorated by a heavy Greek Key, this vegetable tureen was formed in the **Plain Uplift** *shape that was so popular in the 1870s. It was known as* **Olympic Shape** *by Elsmore & Forster. Photograph: Groff.*

No.
194194

Athenia. J. T. Close, registered 1866. The 8″ sugar bowl was potted by W. Adams.

Athena Shape. On the three plates I have seen, there has been no potter's name. The registry date is 1865.

Laurel Wreath. Registered April 4, 1867, by Elsmore & Forster. Detail of the wreath that decorates side and the twisted rope finial. Some pieces of this pattern are found as **Victory Shape.**

Laurel Wreath pieces potted by Elsmore & Forster. Owned by Mrs. Jane Diemer, Delaware. Photograph: Diemer.

These **Laurel Wreath** white ironstone pieces, embellished with portraits of Washington, are very collectible. Potted by Elsmore & Forster as commemorative pieces for the first centennial, they are owned by John and Shirley Anderson. Photograph: H. Phillips.

Athens Shape. Podmore Walker & Co., registry date 1842. Nicknamed **Fleur de lis,** this pattern was sometimes marked Wedgwood & Co., the name of the above firm after 1860.

*Stylized acanthus leaves form the edge of this **Athens Shape** tureen by Wedgwood & Co. Photograph: Groff.*

15 Changes in the Ironstone Scene

White ironstone china potted during the 1860s was carefully impressed with naturalistic grains, grapes, flowers, and leaves. Because styles seemed to shift completely at least every twenty years, we can see definite trends.

The first pattern in this section is nicknamed *Eagle.* It was registered in 1869 and decorated with eagle finials and the thumbprints that had been widely used in the 1860s. After 1891, other animal decorations were used. Examples are the lion heads in *Royal,*

Eagle Dove, or Diamond and Thumbprint are nicknames of this unique shape. These pieces potted by Gelson Bros. Collection of Gary and Carol Grove, Pennsylvania.

dolphin heads in *Victory,* the elephant motif on *Jumbo* handles, and a *Fox* and *Grape* decoration. (See Chapter twelve.)

There were a few patterns that decorated most of the bodies in the 1870s and 1880s. They included *Seashore* and *Budded Vine.* Most of the dishes, though, had plain, simple lines.

During these years, square and rectangular shapes were designed. Perhaps the earliest was the intricate *Seashore Shape,* followed by the *Square Ridged* and *Bamboo* shapes, the *Block Optic, Shaw's Basketweave,* and the nearly square *Favorite* pieces created by W. H. Grindley. Grindley used this same body for colored sets, including brown or blue *Daffodil* transfers, the colored *Moss Rose, Copper Tea Leaf,* and the popular brown and white *Spring* pattern. Made for the first time were square and rectangular butter dishes, butter pats, saucedishes, and platters. The square, nested, open servers, especially those displaying "ladyfinger" ribs, have become collectible both for use and display.

The great majority of white ironstone during the era was made with plain round or oval bodies. They were sometimes named and usually were individualized by handle details. Best known and most potted by both English and American firms, the *Cable and Ring* was used extensively on plain shapes with a little variation in the motifs. Some of these late sets are graceful, while others can only be termed mediocre. Certainly these durable dishes were purchased for everyday use in homes all across America.

By law, after 1891, all imports had to be clearly marked as to the country of their origin. This helps us as we try to date nineteenth-century china. The last few pages of this chapter picture a return to more detailed decorations on the lighter-weight white ironstone sets sold during the closing years of the century. The decor was not as deeply impressed, nor were the designs as naturalistic. Curves and swirls in patterns such as *Tracery* by Johnson Bros. are found on the bodies of turn-of-the-century toilet sets made both by the English and by the rapidly improving American potteries.

By the time a foreign import had to be clearly stamped with its source, most Staffordshire potteries had forsaken the production of inexpensive white wares except for hotel ware. They already were busily engaged in offering finer china bodies to tempt the American buyers.

As the Victorian Age accelerated, American women avidly purchased semiporcelain and porcelain, both flowered and gilded, sent from England to the beauty-starved American housewife. By the turn of the century, the dream of owning the translucent china from Germany, Austria, or Bavaria touched most American homes. The general attitude was, "To be good, china must be imported."

Eagle bowl and pitcher, potted around 1870 by Gelson Bros., is owned by the Diemers in Delaware. Photograph: Diemer.

Eagle. Gelson Bros., registered in 1869, may have been designed with the 1876 centennial in mind. This pattern has also been called **Dove** or **Diamond and Thumbprint.**

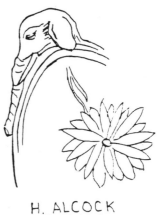

Jumbo. Henry Alcock. The plain, pear-shaped body is characteristic of most 1880s patterns.

Jumbo pitcher, named for the elephant head on the handle. Owned by Mr. and Mrs. John Black. Photograph: Black.

Royal or **Lion's Head.** Other collectors have tagged this design **Ram's Head** but the animal head looks to me like it was taken right off the king of the jungle. Potted by John Edwards, registered 1877.

Victory. John Edwards. Serving dishes were square with rounded corners. The nickname **Dolphin** is often used.

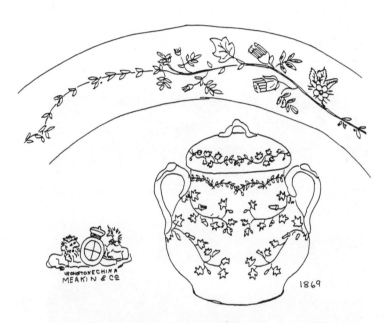

Budded Vine. Meakin & Co., some pieces marked Meakin Bros. This pattern reflects the body decorations of the 1860s on the body lines of the 1870s and 1880s.

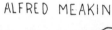

ALFRED MEAKIN

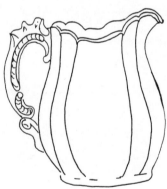

Chelsea. Alfred Meakin, Johnson Bros.

Budded Vine tureen by Meakin & Co. Impressed potting date, 1888. Main lines of the body are like the plain dishes potted in the 1880s. Collection of Jean Hogg, New York. Photograph: Blair.

Seashore Shape. W. E. Corn, after-1868 registry descernible on all pieces I have seen, but in each, the letter designating the year is not clear.

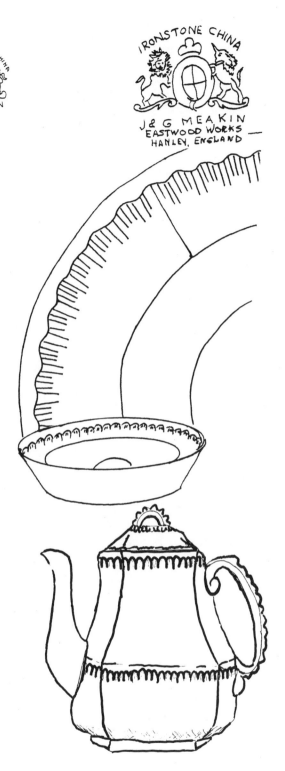

Piecrust. J. & G. Meakin, H. Alcock.

Seashore toilet set pieces owned by the Hoggs of Canajoharie, New York, potted by W. & E. Corn. The lines of the toothbrush holder, soap dish, and pitcher are generally rectangular. From an exhibit at the Fort Plain Museum, Fort Plain, New York. Photograph: Blair.

CHARLES MEAKIN

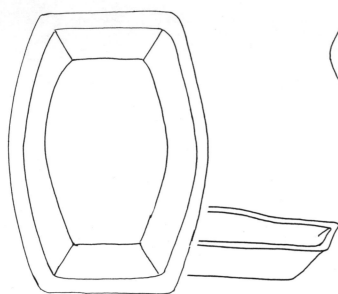

Curved Rectangle. Charles Meakin.

WEDGWOOD & CO.

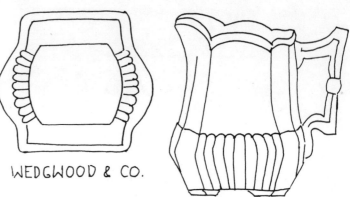

Square Ridged. Wedgwood & Co., Henry Burgess, W. & E. Corn, Mellor, Taylor & Co., H. Alcock & Co.

Square Ridged collection by Johnson Bros., last decades of the nineteenth century. Owned by Mr. and Mrs. John Black, New York. Photograph: Black.

Gentle Square. Thomas Furnival & Sons, circa 1876.

Bamboo. Registered in 1873 by John Edwards, Alfred Meakin, W. H. Grindley.

Square Melon-Ribbed *nest of servers with scalloped edges over melon-shaped ribs by J. & G. Meakin. Other companies, both English and American, made similar sets offering even more sizes. Collection of Mr. and Mrs. John Black. Photograph: Black.*

Block Optic *family jug reunion. All potted by J. & G. Meakin. Collection of the Blacks. Photograph: Black.*

Maddock's **Simplicity** *is a good example of simple designs of the 1870s and 1880s. Most covered vegetables were oval, and most soap dishes were round.* **Simplicity** *was made in both shapes, but the server shown is round and the soap dish is oval. From the collection of Stephen and Silvia Wetherbee, New York. Photograph: Blair.*

Border of Leaves. J. & G. Meakin. This pattern is lightly impressed.

Favorite Shape. W. H. Grindley. This was used as the body for several colored ironstone patterns.

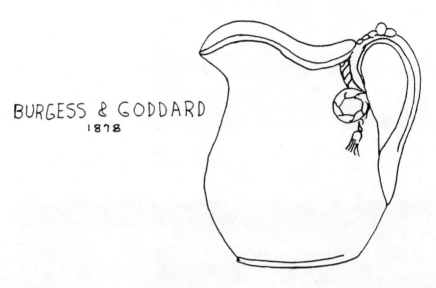

BURGESS & GODDARD
1878

Bow and Tassel. Burgess & Goddard, registered 1878.

CLEMENTSON BROS.

MADDOCK & GATER

Plain Uplift. Maddock & Gater, Clementson Bros., and many others.

Plain Uplift *pieces, exemplifying lines of the 1870s and 1880s. Bodies are heavy at bottom, with handles that seem to lift upward. Tops have acorn finials. Each piece was made by a different potter.*

J.&G. MEAKIN

16 OZ.

BURGESS & GODDARD

UNMARKED

Plain. J. & G. Meakin, Burgess & Goddard, and most Staffordshire potters of the 1870s and 1880s.

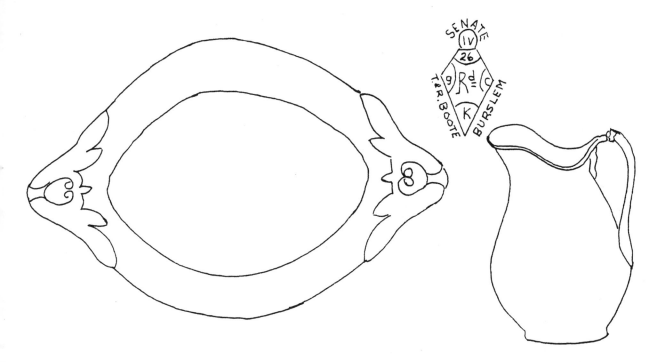

Senate. T. & R. Boote, registered 1870.

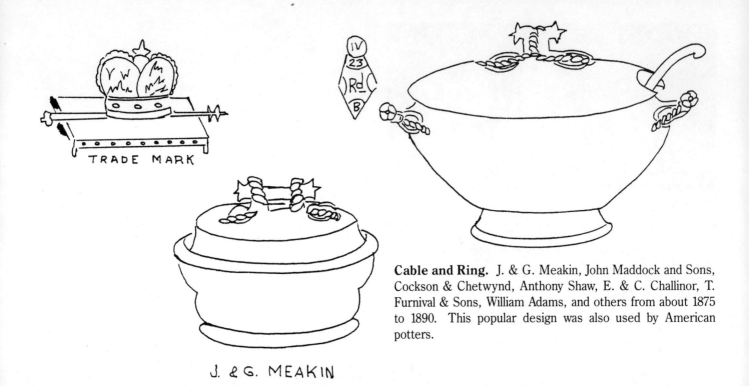

TRADE MARK

J. & G. MEAKIN

Cable and Ring. J. & G. Meakin, John Maddock and Sons, Cockson & Chetwynd, Anthony Shaw, E. & C. Challinor, T. Furnival & Sons, William Adams, and others from about 1875 to 1890. This popular design was also used by American potters.

Handle Details, Plain Bodies

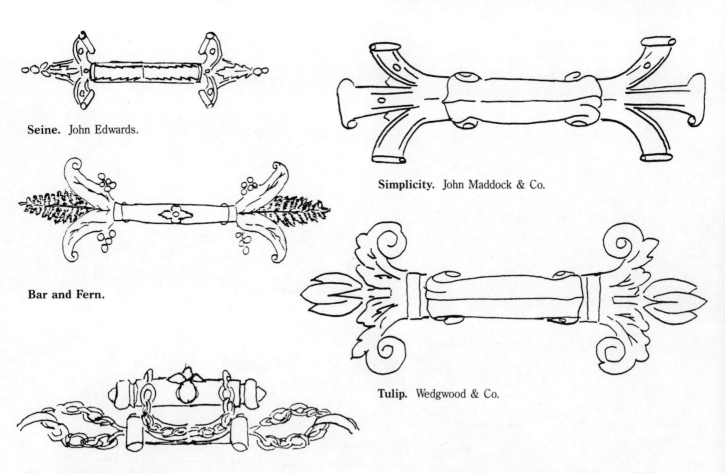

Seine. John Edwards.

Bar and Fern.

Bar and Chain. John Maddock & Co.

Simplicity. John Maddock & Co.

Tulip. Wedgwood & Co.

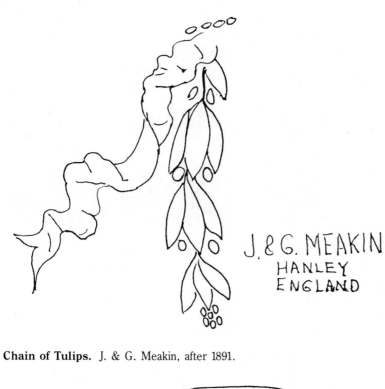

Chain of Tulips. J. & G. Meakin, after 1891.

Fuchsia with Band. Mellor, Taylor & Co., after 1891.

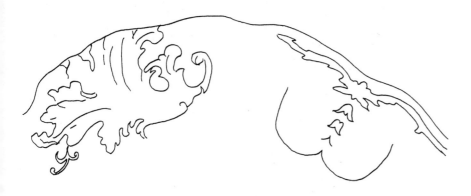

Tracery. Johnson Bros., after 1891.

Tracery. Large turn-of-the-century sugar bowl and creamer potted by Johnson Bros. Collection of Karl and Linda Dalenberg, Massachusetts.

Chrysanthemum. Unmarked shaving mug, with the flowing design of many turn-of-the-century toilet sets.

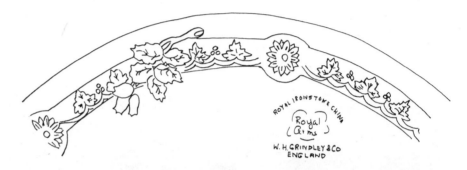

Flower Garden Border. W. H. Grindley & Co., after 1891.

Plain lines of compote complement the pure lines of a jardiniere potted by Alfred Meakin after 1891.

Miniature Scroll. J. & C. Meakin, after 1891.

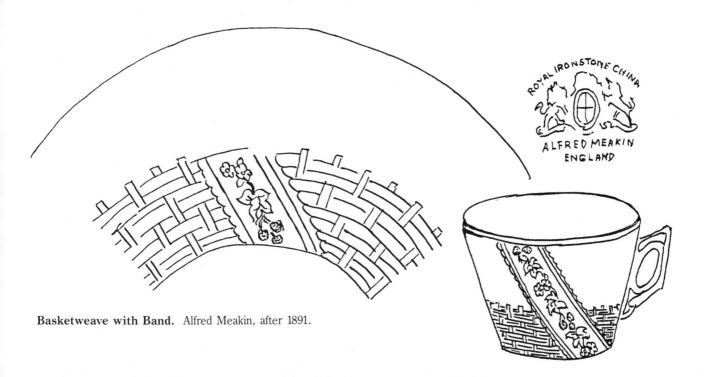

Basketweave with Band. Alfred Meakin, after 1891.

Plain white ironstone is attractively arranged on pumpkin pine table. Surplus pieces are stored in old pine jelly cupboard. Photograph: LeBel.

16   Relish Dishes

This chapter contains line drawings of the shapes used for small servers, which dispensed conserves, pickles, relishes, nuts, or candies. Some collectors employ the servers for buffet meals, while others serve tossed salads on a variety of dishes.

The leaf and shell shapes were used by the English potters of the late eighteenth and early nineteenth centuries on breakfast or tea services. One dessert set often would have two or three leaf-shaped dishes, some of which were pedestalled. Rarely, we come across a pedestalled white ironstone doughnut stand that matches the design of a relish dish.

Occasionally relish dishes of the same pattern were made in several sizes. I have seen the 1851 *Scallop* and the *Grenade Shape,* both by Boote, in at least two different lengths.

The decoration on some of these small dishes has no relation to the pattern name marked on the bottom. For example, the lines of the relish dish stamped *Sydenham Shape* are not at all related to the lines on *Sydenham* sets of china. *Columbia Shape* sets contained and marked a shape similar to the *Sydenham,* and J. Clementson potted an almost matching piece. Often, we are forced to make an educated guess from the registry marks or the general lines. Some patterns are clearly stamped, or else we recognize the motifs—especially those used in the 1860s and 1870s. We are sure, nonetheless, that early white ironstone sets included three or four relish dishes.

Collectors are fascinated by the wide variation of shapes. When our cupboards overflow with gleaming white, we'll still find some small area or high shelf to display these interestingly molded forms.

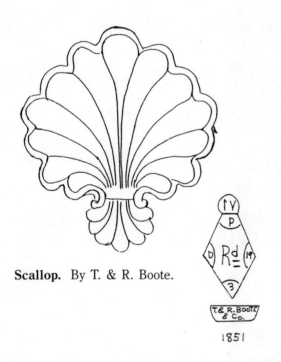

Scallop. By T. & R. Boote.

Large center server and four small individual servers. All marked T. &. R. Boote, 1851, to go with the **Boote's 1851 Octagon** *dishes. Same registry date.*

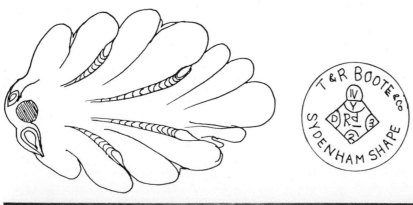

Three related relish dishes. Top left: **Columbia.** *Bottom left:* **Sydenham** *by Clementson. Right: Boote's* **Sydenham.** *Photograph: W. Wetherbee.*

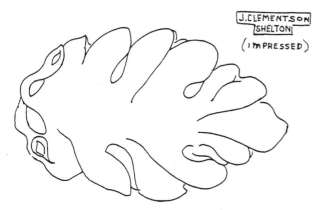

Sydenham or **Columbia.** This shape was used for the relish dishes sold with these two patterns. This particular dish was made by Clementson.

Star Flower. J. W. Pankhurst.

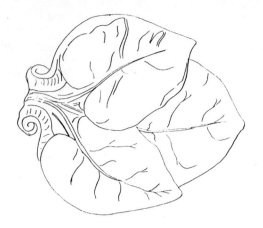

Pond Lily Pad. Jas. Edwards.

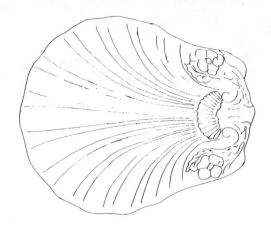

Shell and Flower. Potter not marked.

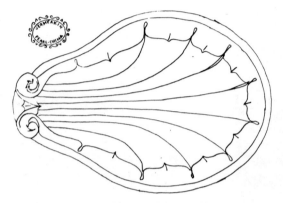

Pearl Sydenham. J. & G. Meakin.

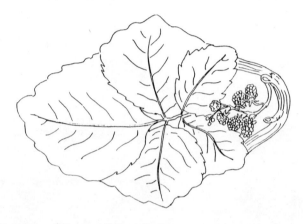

Potomac Shape. Baker & Co.

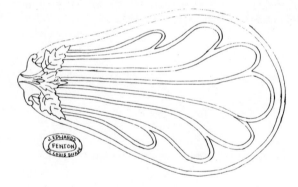

St. Louis Shape. John Edwards.

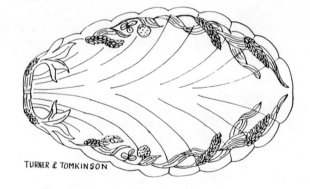

Wheat and Clover. Turner & Tomkinson.

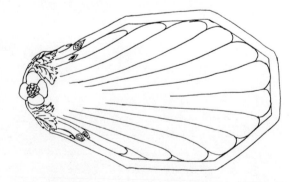

Prize Bloom. T. J. & J. Mayer.

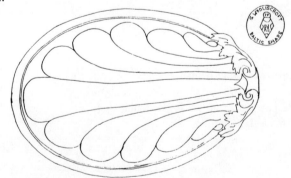

Baltic Shape. G. Wooliscroft.

MEAKIN BROS. & CO.
COBRIDGE

JAS. EDWARDS & SONS
DALEHALL

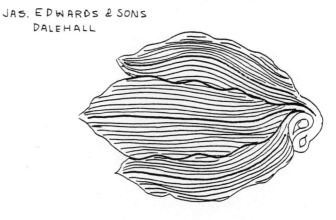

Budded Vine.   Meakin Bros. & Co.

Husk.   Jas. Edwards & Sons.

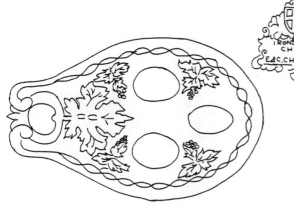

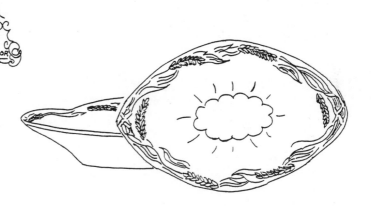

Vintage Shape.   E. & C. Challinor.

Wheat.   J. & G. Meakin.

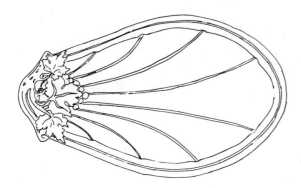

J. & G. MEAKIN

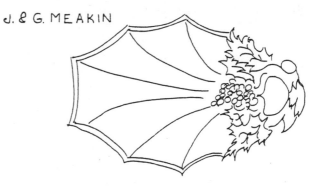

Panelled Grape.   J.F.

Fruit of the Vine.   J. & G. Meakin.

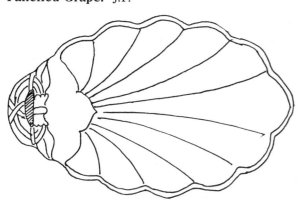

Gothic.   Registered 1852 by J. Wedgwood.

Wreath of Leaves.   Potter unknown.

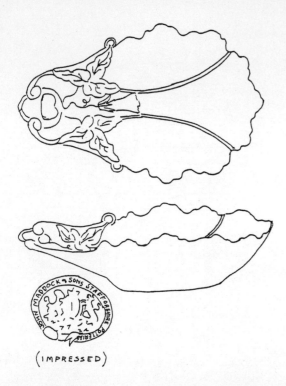

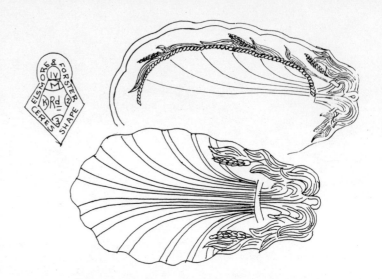

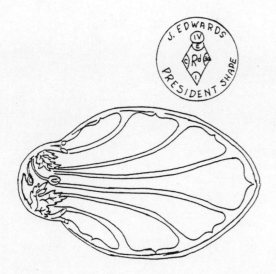

Ceres. Elsmore & Forster, registered 1859. These dishes are found both with and without the cable, and are clearly marked "Ceres," E. & F.

Lined Glory. John Maddock & Sons.

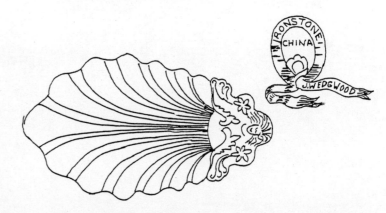

Early Cameo. J. Wedgwood, Davenport, registered 1848.

JAMES EDWARDS
DALEHALL

CIRCA 1848

President Shape. J. Edwards.

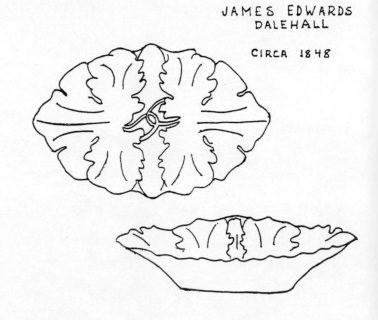

Double Leaf. James Edwards, Barrow & Co.

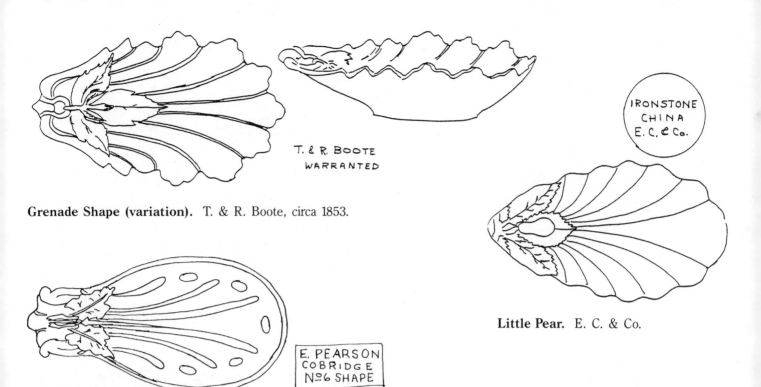

Grenade Shape (variation). T. & R. Boote, circa 1853.

Little Pear. E. C. & Co.

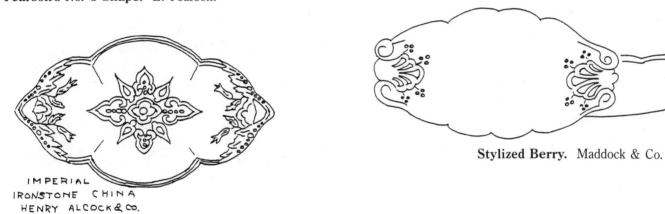

Pearson's No. 6 Shape. E. Pearson.

Stylized Berry. Maddock & Co.

Stylized Flower. Henry Alcock & Co. After 1861.

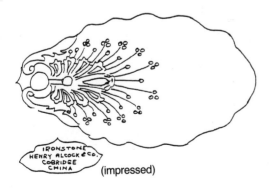

Floral Ray. Henry Alcock & Co. After 1861. Impressed mark.

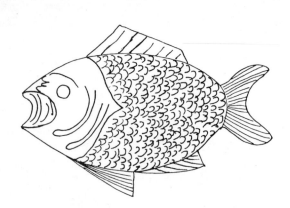

Fish Dish. Unmarked.

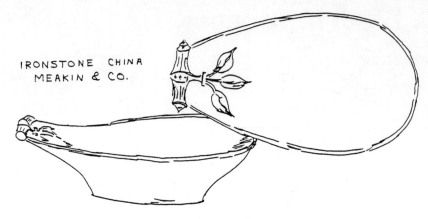

IRONSTONE CHINA
MEAKIN & CO.

Plain. Meakin & Co. Typical of the 1870s and 1880s.

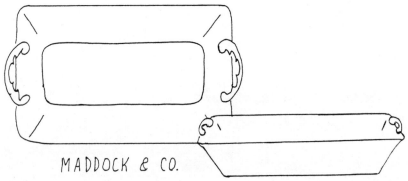

MADDOCK & CO.

Simple Rectangle. Maddock & Co.

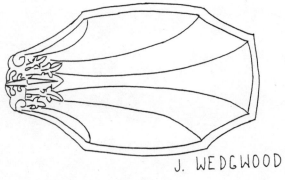

J. WEDGWOOD

Angled Leaf. J. Wedgwood.

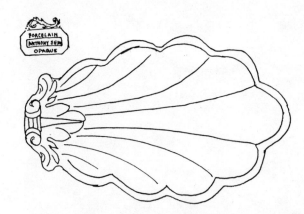

PORCELAIN
ANTHONY SHAW
OPAQUE

De Soto Shape. Thos. Hughes, A. Shaw. These dishes are very deep and shell-like.

17 The Copper Tea Leaf Story

There exists a dedicated group of ironstone collectors whose loyalties are undivided. They search avidly for the white dishes bedecked with a copper band and a copper tea leaf motif.

No one is quite sure where this "tea leaf" design originated, but Anthony Shaw is credited with the first use of the well-known glowing copper leaves and attached band. Certainly the motif does not look like the real tea leaf; in fact, the leaf and bud remind us of a strawberry plant. Early advertisements listed it as *Lustre Band with Sprig* or *Lustre Spray*. Twentieth-century collectors probably christened this pattern *Copper Tea Leaf*, and that is how it is still identified.

Anthony Shaw was the first to use two shapes that had already been potted in all-white ironstone in an earlier decade. The "blanks" of these two early and difficult-to-locate true Copper Tea Leaf shapes are drawn below. We nickname them *Fan* and *Shaw's Hanging Leaves*.

A.SHAW

Shaw added these special decorations to his well-known *Chinese Shape*, his *Bordered Fuchsia*, and his *Lily-of-the-Valley*. The tea leaves are sometimes found inside the bottoms of cups and waste bowls.

In the 1870s, 1880s, and 1890s, Shaw and his partners used this decor on most of their patterns, including *Cable and Ring*, a *Sunburst* hexagon form, and square, oval, and round bodies. We can pinpoint the date of a well potted, plain Shaw service to just before the turn of the century.

Collectors of this well-known pattern rely on the different underglaze base colors, such as dark green, black, or purple, as an aid to identification. The underglaze application was a guide for the artist, who later added the gilt. In later years, the gilt often wore off. Potters must have struggled before they finally perfected a copper lustre finish that would endure. By the late 1870s, most Staffordshire firms used a permanent underglaze copper lustre on white ironstone that the housewife could use without fear that the glow would disappear.

Here is an incomplete list of other English Shapes used as blanks for Copper Tea Leaf:

Empress Shape by Adams
Huron Shape by Adams
Feather Border by John Edwards
Pie Crust by H. Alcock
Victory by John Edwards
Rooster Head by Furnival
Cable and Ring by Furnival, Anthony Shaw, Arthur Wilkinson, Henry Burgess, E. & C. Challinor
Favorite by W. H. Grindley
Bamboo by W. H. Grindley, Alfred Meakin, John Edwards
Plain Acanthus by Thomas Hughes
Chelsea by Johnson Bros., Alfred Meakin
Square Ridged by Henry Burgess, W. & E. Corn, Mellor, Taylor & Co., Wedgwood & Co.
Plain Round by W. & E. Corn, Furnival, John Maddock, Alfred Meakin
Plain Square by Mellor, Taylor & Co., Anthony Shaw, Wedgwood & Co., A. Wilkinson

Copper Tea Leaf was brighter and still inexpensive, and was welcomed after years of plain white. The American natives must have clamored for the lustre sprig china. Otherwise, English and American manufacturers would not have supplied it so freely.

A few native potters advertised china sets described as "underglaze Lustre Band and Sprig." In 1881, J. & E. Mayer of the well-known Staffordshire family came to America and opened a pot-bank at Beaver Falls, Pennsylvania. The company guaranteed that their copper lustre decorations on white granite were as "Indestructible as the Rock of Ages!" Working near the East Liverpool pottery area, the Cartright Brothers also made sets of tea leaf ironstone. Other native craftsmen who sold tea leaf were Wm. Brunt Jr. & Co.; Goodwin Bros. Pottery Co.; Knowles, Taylor & Knowles Co.; and C. C. Thompson Co.

During these same years, several potters trimmed table services with a simple copper gilt band without the sprig. Today, these pieces would make an interesting collection. Even the earlier shapes are still available at lower prices. A few of the shapes with this treatment are *Gothic, Augusta, New York, Chinese, Walley's Niagara, Double Sydenham,* and *Ceres.* The Ceres shape, with copper-covered wheat and stalks, is anything but inexpensive.

The Variants

Collectors like to accumulate other copper lustre decorated pieces, which they call CTL variations. Some of these pieces have surpassed the popularity of the more plentiful *Copper Tea Leaf* dishes. Most of these "experimental" motifs were employed before the familiar tea leaf caught on.

The desirable *Fig Cousin* Shape listed elsewhere in this book was potted by Davenport. Each has a pink lustre trim over the impressed flowers and is edged by copper bands and emblazoned with the usual tea leaf sprig.

J. Clementson and his successors used some of their earlier shapes as blanks for their Teaberry sometimes called Coffee Berry) motifs on such bodies as *New York Shape*, *Prairie Shape,* a later *Plain* round, and a later *Square* shape. The underglaze color looks black or dark green where the overglaze copper lustre has worn off. We see more of these pieces marked *Clementson Bros.* than with the original *J. Clementson*. A similar variant applied over the *New York Shape* is a "seaweed" motif.

*Shaw's **1856 Fan**, cream with CTL trim. Armbruster collection. Photograph: Armbruster.*

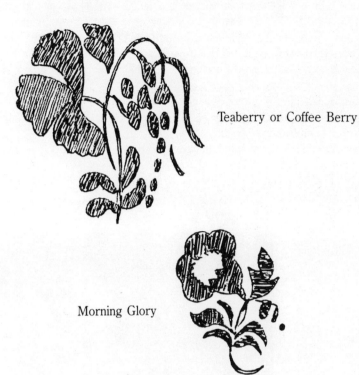

Teaberry or Coffee Berry

Morning Glory

An interesting study can be made of the services offered by Elsmore & Forster in the pre-tea leaf years. The most coveted of their copper-touched dishes had the usual copper band with a branch nicknamed *Morning Glory,* which starred on *Portland Shape, Ceres Shape* and on a *Plain* 1880s shape. In these later years, James F. Wileman had a similar design added to his plain *Richelieu Shape*. Elsmore & Forster also used a *Pepper Leaf* (also called *Tobacco Leaf*) on later plain bodies.

A *Little Scroll* shape made by Elsmore & Forster can be found either with edges in two shades of blue, or with flow-blue edges banded with copper lustre. An 1862 potting date on these services supports the theory that these efforts were forerunners of the more prolific tea leaf.

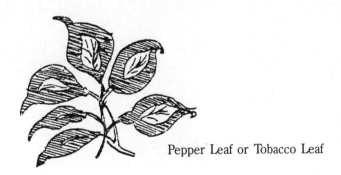

Pepper Leaf or Tobacco Leaf

Elsmore & Forster's 1859 *Ceres Shape,* which was deeply detailed and gleaming white, was an immediate success. Wheat collectors treasure pieces of this pattern that have the added color of copper lustre over the wheat, have two shades of blue, or have green shards between golden heads of wheat. These are most often discovered in the Middle Atlantic states.

A green tea leaf variation was originated by Edward Walley for his *Niagara* and *Gothic* shapes. Jagged three-leaf clovers alternate with a single bud, all of which are tied together around borders and bodies with either a narrow or a wiggly green line.

Powell and Bishop used a triple-leaf gold lustre twig and band on their *Square Ribbed* shape, registered in 1876. This firm also manufactured a service with a "rose" flower on tea leaf with under-lustre green, topped by the usual shining copper on an embossed prairie plate.

This barely introduces the whole subject of *Copper Tea Leaf* ironstone and other related treatments. For in-depth information on the subject, refer to Annise Doring Heaivilin's *Grandma's Tea Leaf Ironstone,* published in 1981.

A Tea Leaf Club International with hundreds of enthusiastic members meets at an annual convention and issues the publication *Tea Leaf Readings* six times a year. Information about the club's activities can be secured by writing to Tea Leaf Readings, 9720 Whiskey Run, Laurel, Maryland 20707.

This collectible treatment of the **Ceres** *pattern by Elsmore & Forster was trimmed with a copper lustre coating over the embossed wheat and shards. Included in the Armbruster Collection. Photograph: Armbruster.*

Chinese Shape *by Shaw with tea leaf design. Many authorities credit Shaw with the first use of this added decoration. Collection of Mr. and Mrs. William Horner, Delaware. Photograph: Dr. Horner.*

Portland Shape *by Elsmore & Forster, with added copper tea leaf lustre decor. Owned by Mr. and Mrs. William Horner. Photograph: Dr. Horner.*

Gold lustre design on a popular style of the 1870s. Footed rectangular shape in the serving pieces accompanied by handled cups with high-walled saucers. Potted by Powell & Bishop in 1876. Collection of Mr. and Mrs. William Horner. Photograph: Dr. Horner.

Three pieces of Copper Tea Leaf on a **Shaw's Lily-of-the-Valley** white blank. The tea leaf motif is in the bottom of the cups and bowl. Collection of Dick and Adele Armbruster. Photograph: Groff.

Milk jug with teaberry and copper band on Clementson's **New York Shape.** Collection of Dick and Adele Armbruster. Photograph: Groff.

New York Shape piece with dark greenish brown trim by Clementson. Oval sugar bowl with light blue trim, accented with cobalt blue, potted 1862, registered by shape in 1856 by Elsmore & Forster. **Ceres** shape with chocolate brown over wheat motif by Elsmore & Forster. All decorated in a manner similar to the later copper tea leaf. Photograph: Blair.

153

Three pieces of **Experimental Tulip** *on a* **Little Scroll** *blank by Elsmore & Forster, potted in the early 1860s. Another treatment on this shape used flow blue on the leaves with an added copper lustre band. Collection of Eileen and Lionel Sirois. Photograph: Blair.*

A great Copper Tea Leaf lustre coffeepot on a **Shaw's Hanging Leaves** *shape. Owned by Dick and Adele Armbruster. Photograph: Armbruster.*

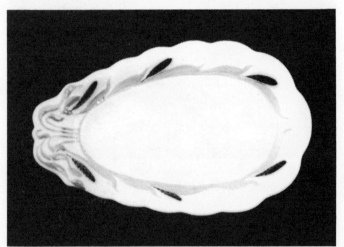

A **Ceres** *relish dish with two tones of added blue. Potted by Elsmore & Forster. Owned by Eileen and Lionel Sirois. Photograph: Groff.*

A pair of **Double Sydenham** *creamers: white by T. Goodfellow and white with copper lustre band by Livesley & Powell. Collection of Ray and Priscilla Casavant. Photograph: Groff.*

One of the favorite "blanks" for **Copper Tea Leaf with Band.** Collection of Julie Rich.

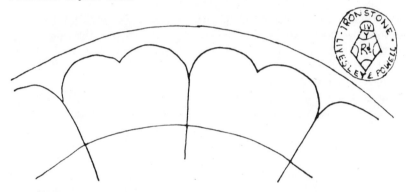

Ring of Hearts. Livesley & Powell. Similar to **Augusta Shape.** Both used as a base for a plain copper band decoration.

Perhaps the most collectible of the Copper Tea Leaf dishes potted by Davenport, who used a pink lustre trim over the leaves and the usual motif over the **Fig Cousin** *shape. Fortunate owners are the Michigan Armbrusters. Photograph: Armbruster.*

Clementson Bros.' **Medallion Scroll** *coffeepot decorated with copper lustre coffee berry. Armbruster collection. Photograph: Armbruster.*

This high reticulated fruit bowl by Anthony Shaw has been found with a copper tea leaf lustre motif inside the bowl. Owned by the Erdmans in Texas. Photograph: Erdman.

Unknown shape with copper lustre Morning Glory motif. Impressed mark: W. Baker & Co., Stone China, Fenton. Owned by the Armbrusters. Photograph: Armbruster.

18 American White Ironstone

Blank for the "presentation" pitchers.

Through history, when man migrated to a new location, one of his first jobs was to shape clay vessels to help sort, store, and cook his food. Later, he molded clay blocks to make shelters.

Crossing the Atlantic in the 1600s, the European colonists followed this familiar pattern, as brick workers and "pott-makers" searched for clay to form bricks and tiles, butter crocks, water coolers, jugs, and bowls. Records indicate that these early potteries were located near Salem, Massachusetts; at New Haven, Connecticut; in Virginia; New Amsterdam; near South Amboy, New Jersey; and later in Georgia and the Carolinas.

During the following one hundred fifty years, American potters supplied the simple wares for daily living. Fragile, inexpensive redware sufficed at first. Gradually, the body was improved and decorated with simple slip designs. Using wheels, potters threw more durable stoneware into the shapes of crocks and jugs. By 1800, most potters advertised Rockingham and yellowware pieces. And during the same era, the simple sponged wares that are so collectible today helped brighten tables and cupboards.

Meanwhile, British potteries shipped quantities of china to the New World and sold cheaply to the American homeowners. Native craftsmen did not have the skill to compete, nor could they produce at such a low cost. A few qualified potters produced fine dishes after the American Revolution, but most companies survived for short periods only.

In the late 1700s, Josiah Wedgwood wrote of the colonies, "They have every material there, equal if not superior to our own for carrying on that manfacture." On the American continent, there were inexhaustible resources for the china maker, including endless stores of rich kaolin (the fine, white pipe clay first used by the Cherokees), many other kinds of clay, earths in Alabama, lithomarge in Tennessee, and unknown resources in the ground of the Far West.

By the middle of the nineteenth century, the population was less mobile. Ready markets were found in every American city and on the farms that dotted the countryside. Finally, then, the native potters began in earnest to produce American-made dishes.

White graniteware was made in most American potteries from about 1860 to 1900. At first, simple patterns and methods were copied from the Staffordshire potters in England. The finer processes, however, were closely guarded secrets passed down generation by generation in England. Much American experimentation was necessary.

Jersey City Pottery was founded in 1829. This firm was taken over by Rouse & Turner who, soon after 1850, began to mark whitewares with the English coat of arms in the hopes of capturing some of the market used by the English.

City Pottery of Trenton claimed to be the first company to manufacture white granite in the New Jersey pottery center outside Trenton. This firm received a medal from the New Jersey Agricultural Society for best white graniteware.

The Bennington potters of Vermont were quite aware of the huge imports of all-white ironstone from England in the late 1840s and 1850s. In their United States Pottery Co., J. & E. Norton potted white granitewares from 1850 to 1858.

Norton's well-known "sweetheart" or "presentation" pitchers had a white ironstone base decorated with flowers and gilt. Since so many are initialled or emblazoned with the recipient's name, it seems that each was made to order. This same plain white shape was copied by other American potters in the next decades.

Shortly after Boote registered its popular *Sydenham* pattern, the Nortons used similar lines in gray-white toilet sets that included waste jars and large footed tubs. Norton also made white ironstone escutcheons, inkwells, keyhole covers, paperweights, and mugs. Their beautiful Parian jugs were covered completely with sculptured designs. A few of these, executed in white ironstone, are coveted today.

These Bennington potters are best known for their single pieces and complete coffee and tea services in flint enamel, Rockingham glazes, and Parian wares.

Vermont potters and others marketed gold-bordered white porcelain dinner sets in the familiar lines of the *Gothic* patterns. Today it is impossible to prove origins, but these sets are undoubtedly American, since similar contemporary English china was carefully marked.

Collectors who want to identify early Bennington white graniteware should consult the well-illustrated *Bennington Pottery and Porcelain* by Richard Carter Barret.

Wm. Brunt Jr. & Co. claimed to have made the first whitewares near the East Liverpool, Ohio, pottery area. Other writers credit John Wyllie as being the first to make ironstone china west of the Alleghenies. Wyllie and his son left Pittsburgh and moved to the East Liverpool settlement, where they purchased the two-kiln pottery of Brunt & Hill and re-equipped it for making whiteware in 1874.

Knowles, Taylor, & Knowles drew its first kiln of whiteware in 1872. This firm made a good grade of ironstone china. By 1886, it was outproducing all other American potteries, employed five hundred men and women, used fifteen tons of clay a day, and turned out a crate of ware every ten minutes.

By 1879, eight East Liverpool potteries were making stone china. At first, items were either unmarked or else marked to make the purchaser think he was buying an English import.

Most of the potteries making whitewares received some of their knowledge from Staffordshire men who had emigrated to America. The J. & E. Mayer Co. of Beaver Falls, Pennsylvania, and Thomas Maddock & Sons of Trenton, New Jersey, came from well-known pottery families in England.

It was difficult and expensive to change a pot works so that whitewares, as well as yellowware and Rockingham, could be made. The potters had to raise the necessary capital, learn new methods, hire workers with better skills, and sell their products in a market already flooded with good ceramics from Great Britain.

A relative of the Meakin potters came to work in the East Liverpool potteries. He helped Knowles, Taylor, & Knowles to convert their pot works so that whiteware could be manufactured. He also helped convert at least eight other plants for production of white granite in this pottery area.

As the Industrial Revolution moved across America, the ceramics workers became alert to new ideas that would speed production and improve their products. In the 1860s, gas-fired potteries were first used. The old charcoal and coal-fired kilns, with their smoke and ash, had often discolored china. The new fuel resulted in better dishes. The American potter ceased to use the potter's wheel, and geared machinery helped grind clay to to fine powder. Firms had to go farther afield to find the proper clays for the white bodies. A few pieces, such as a crooked bowl or wobbly teapot, remind us of the early struggle of these native craftsmen.

When American potters were struggling to capture a portion of the native china market, they sometimes resorted to marking their wares so that the housewife would think she was buying an import. A few marks look almost exactly like the Royal Arms at first glance. One example of this is a mark stamped by the Glasgow Pottery Co., Trenton, New Jersey. It appears to be the English Arms, except that its monogram replaced the quartered decoration within the shield. The old majestic lion reclines just as proudly as ever, and the fabulous unicorn prances on. Other marks more subtly implied English origins by using anchor, feather, crown, or circled motifs. Old records reveal that some orders for white American table services were specifically requested to be left unmarked.

By the 1870s, ceramics in America had begun to come of age. The silversmiths, potters of useful crockery, and molders of glassware had already marketed goods that rivaled similar English products. The chief chinaware manufacturers in America worked around the potting centers near Trenton, New Jersey, and East Liverpool, Ohio. As our country's first centennial approached, a new pride in American-made products increased. The United States government reinforced this feeling by inaugurating a decade of high tariffs—up to 50 percent on imported ceramic wares. As a result, native potters were challenged to produce china that was acceptable to the American housewife, who had always thought good china had to be imported.

In January 1875 at Philadelphia, seventy representatives of the National Association of Potters agreed not to copy patterns from other countries. They also agreed to enter exhibits of native work in the Centennial Exhibition the following year.

Despite the second resolution, the ceramics exhibit was almost hidden at the exhibition and attracted little attention. Examples of potters' crafts were displayed by the Trenton, Philadelphia, and New York potters, but there were few entries from the Ohio firms. Wares attracting attention were those of the New York City Pottery, Ott & Brewer, Union Porcelain Works, and Homer Laughlin of East Liverpool. A white graniteware "Daily Bread" platter was shown by the Trenton Pottery Co.

Another Philadelphia Centennial exhibitor that was noticed was the St. Johns Chinaware Co. from St. Johns, Quebec, located about twenty-three miles southeast of Montreal. This was the first pottery in Canada to concentrate on the production of whiteware. It had begun potting in 1874 under the leadership of Farrars, who had migrated from New England. At first he had difficulty finding skilled potters who knew how to work with whitewares. Finally, he was compelled to employ Staffordshire men for more than half of the work force in his pottery.

The ironstone made by the St. Johns Stone Chinaware Co. was inexpensive, well-made china, some of which was decorated with gilt and flowers. Some all-white dishes marked by this company were in the *Wheat and Blackberry, Wheat,* and *Scallop* patterns. St. Johns also potted sets shaped in white ironstone and decorated with blue transfer designs in the Staffordshire manner.

Most of the American sets of white ironstone china were plain, with a little design in relief. The English pattern *Cable and Ring* was also made by Greenwood Pottery Co., Cook and Hancock, and American Crockery Co. Wheat motifs and rectangular and square shapes were often used. The potters were struggling with the textures of the clay itself, with the purity of the white color, and with the smoothness of the glazes. Collectors can easily gather a group of utilitarian wares of American ironstone, including spittoons, invalid feeders, milk pans, mush bowls, "pig" bed warmers, footed tubs, wine coolers, and nests of servers.

Rarely, we fine unusual pieces of American white ironstone, or white granite, as it was often advertised. A few detailed comports were of good design. Of course, all the Bennington graniteware has become desirable. The most popular collectible has become the "Daily Bread" platters, both marked and unmarked. Almost every firm shaped these oval servers, decorated them with wheat, and varied the wording. Most slogans began with "Give Us This Day" on one border and concluded the quote on the opposite side, "Our Daily Bread." Others admonished "Waste Not—Want Not." Some advised "Where Reason Rules—The Appetite Obeys." I have seen these platters marked with the following: T. P. Works (Trenton Pottery Co.); J. M. & Co. (Glasgow Pottery Co.); M. P. & Co.; O. P. & Co. (Onondaga Pottery Co.); John Wyllie & Son; and St. Johns, P. Q.

When American pottery firms had mastered the techniques required to produce acceptable whitewares, they continued to improve as they practiced good ceramics engineering. The heavy white ware made the firms solvent, but the potters still longed to create beautiful porcelain and bone china that could rival the European chinas.

The last fifteen years of the nineteenth century saw great strides in the quality of American chinaware. By 1900, Americans were proud to declare, "We made it in America!"

American Potters of White Ironstone

* Exhibited in the Philadelphia Centennial Exposition of 1876.

Firm and Location	Marks	Date Founded
Alpaugh & Magowan Empire Pottery New Jersey	A. & M.	1884
American China Co. Toronto, Ohio		1897
American Crockery Co. Trenton, New Jersey	English arms A.C. Co.	1876
Anchor Pottery Trenton, New Jersey	Modified English arms with AP monogram in center	1894
L. B. Beerbower & Co. Elizabeth, New Jersey	STONE CHINA	1879
Beerbower & Griffin Phoenix Pottery Phoenixville, Pennsylvania	Arms of state of Pennsylvania and, in circle, initials B & G.	1867
Edwin Bennett Pottery Co. Baltimore, Maryland	E. B. Phoenix	1860
Wm. Brunt Pottery Co. East Liverpool, Ohio	W.B.P. Co.	1894
Burgess & Campbell International Pottery Co. New Jersey	Circle with rampaut lion, Burgess & Campbell	1879
Burroughs & Mountford Trenton, New Jersey	B. & M.	1879
* City Pottery Co. Trenton, New Jersey	Shield C.P. Co.	1859
Cartwright & Co. East Liverpool, Ohio		1864
Chelsea China Co. New Cumberland, West Virginia	Star, crescent moon, and Chelsea White Granite	1888
Cook & Hancock Crescent Pottery New Jersey	Cook & Hancock	1881

Coxon & Co. Empire Pottery Trenton, New Jersey	Badge with eagle in center and ribbon beneath with name of firm	1863
Crown Pottery Co. Evansville, Indiana	English arms with C.P.C. monogram in center	1891
Messrs. Dale & Davis Prospect Hill Pottery Trenton, New Jersey		1880
East Liverpool Pottery Co. East Liverpool, Ohio	E.L.P. Co.	1881
East Trenton Pottery Co. Trenton, New Jersey	E.T.P. Co. New Jersey seal also English	White granite by 1888
Eagle Pottery Co. Trenton, New Jersey		
* Etruria Pottery Trenton, New Jersey (subsequently Ott & Brewer)	Etruria Pottery	1863
Fell & Thropp Co. Trenton, New Jersey	English arms F.&T. Co.	——
Globe Pottery Co. East Liverpool, Ohio	Globe Pottery Co.	1881
Goodwin Pottery Co. East Liverpool, Ohio		1876
Greenwood Pottery Trenton, New Jersey	C.P. Co. Greenwood China (after 1886)	c. 1860
Harker Pottery Co. East Liverpool, Ohio	Horizontal bow with vertical arrow, H.P. Co.	1879
D. F. Haynes & Co. Chesapeake Pottery Baltimore, Maryland		1879
Joseph Jager Peoria Pottery Co. Peoria, Illinois	P.P. Co.	Early 1870s
Jersey City Pottery Jersey City, New Jersey (subsequently Rouse & Turner)		1829
Edwin M. Knowles China Co. Newell, West Virginia		1872
Knowles, Taylor & Knowles East Liverpool, Ohio	K.T. & K.	1872

* Homer Laughlin & Co. East Liverpool, Ohio	HOMER LAUGHLIN	1879
* Thomas Maddock & Sons Eagle Pottery Trenton, New Jersey	EAGLE POTTERY	1869
Maryland Pottery Co. Baltimore, Maryland	Circular eagle, MARYLAND POTTERY CO. (seal of Maryland after 1883)	1881
Mayer Pottery Co. Beaver Falls, Pennsylvania	Square enclosing a circle with WARRANTED STONE CHINA J.&.E. MAYER	1881
D. E. McNichol Pottery Co. East Liverpool, Ohio		1882
Mellor & Co. Cook Pottery Co. New Jersey	MELLOR & CO.	——
Mercer Pottery Co. Trenton, New Jersey	Double shield MERCER POTTERY CO.	1868
Millington & Astbury Pottery Trenton, New Jersey	M.A.P.	1853 Whiteware after 1861
Morley & Co. Wellsville Pottery Co.	M. & Co.	1879
* Messrs. Morrison & Carr New York City Pottery New York, New York		1860
* John Moses & Co. (Glasgow Pottery Co.) Trenton, New Jersey	Eagle over shield, J.M. & Co.	1863
New England Pottery Co. East Boston, Massachusetts	Seal of state of Massachusetts from 1878 to 1883, N.E.P. Co.	1854
Onondaga Pottery Co. Syracuse, New York	Arms of New York, O.P. Co.	1871
* Peoria Pottery Co. Peoria, Illinois	English arms (no initials) WARRANTED	1873
Phoenixville Pottery Co. Phoenixville, Pennsylvania		1867

Potter's Cooperative Co. East Liverpool, Ohio	DRESDEN	1876
Rouse & Turner (formerly Jersey City Pott.) Jersey City, New Jersey	R.&T.	Before 1850
St. Johns Stone Chinaware Co. St. Johns, Province of Quebec, Canada	English arms, ST. JOHNS, P. Q.	1874
Steubenville Pottery Co. Steubenville, Ohio	S. P. Co., others	1879
Stephen Tams & Co. Trenton, New Jersey		1861
Trenton China Co. Trenton, New Jersey		1859
Trenton Pottery Co. Trenton, New Jersey	T.P. CO. CHINA	1865
Union Pottery Co. Trenton, New Jersey		1880
United States Pottery Co. Bennington, Vermont		1849
Vance Faience Pottery Tiltonville, Ohio		1880
Vodrey & Brothers	Monogram V over B	1879
Warwick China Co. Wheeling, West Virginia		1877
Wheeling Pottery Co. Wheeling, West Virginia	STONE CHINA	1879
Willets Manufacturing Co. Trenton, New Jersey	W.M. Co.	1879
John Wyllie & Sons Great Western Pottery East Liverpool, Ohio	Double shield of English and U.S. seals, J.W. & SON	1874

A half-dozen pieces of American made ironstone, typical of early native potting in white graniteware. Unmarked except for square dish in center bottom, which is marked with a printed "91" (probably 1891) over arms circling a monogram in a shield. Photograph: Blair.

Several American potteries made these melon-ribbed compotes in various sizes. Unmarked.

Unmarked American pieces: Square sugar box and mustard cups decorated with a three-dimensional face similar to **Gothic Cameo**. Photograph: Blair.

A group of American-made utilitarian pieces. Top: Onondaga Pottery Co., spittoon with colonial profile cameo decoration, and another spittoon with gargoyle design. Bottom: unmarked chamber pot, hand spittoon in one piece, hand spittoon in two pieces marked "1866 Nat. Home for Volunteer Soldiers." Collection of Mr. and Mrs. John Black. Photograph: Black.

*Sharply molded wheat on a round **Daily Bread Platter** by Onondaga Pottery Co. Collection of Florence Travis. Photograph: Blair.*

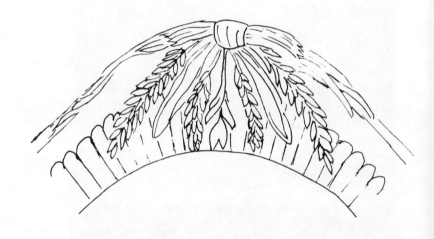

Decorated with small ribs with wheat handles, this bread tray is not marked. Photograph: Blair.

*Two **Daily Bread Platters** from the same mold. The transfer decoration is a light navy blue. The initials under the usual arms are blurred. Photograph: Blair.*

Daily Bread Platter. *Highly collectible dish made of white ironstone by American potters. Most included a wheat motif, as did this one by Onondaga Pottery Co. Owned by James and Doris Walker. Photograph: Blair.*

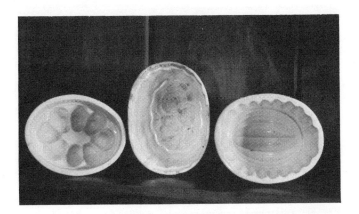

Pudding molds, usually unmarked, were often potted by American firms. Owned by the Hoggs in New York. Photograph: Blair.

Part of a nest of heart-and-leaf decorated bowls for the kitchen. American potter. Photograph: Groff.

*A miniature set edged in blue, potted by an American firm, unmarked. Teapot is **Little Scroll** by Elsmore & Forster. Owned by Eileen Sirois. Photograph: Groff.*

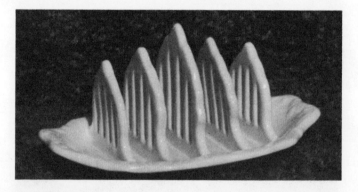

Unmarked toast holder graced a breakfast table in the nineteenth century. Photograph: Black.

Different indeed is this wall holder for both toothbrushes and soap. Unmarked. Photograph: Black.

Draped Leaf (B) *by James Edwards next to late, miniature, unmarked tea set. Cups to this set were handled.*

Rare American-made mustard jar. No mark. Photograph: Groff.

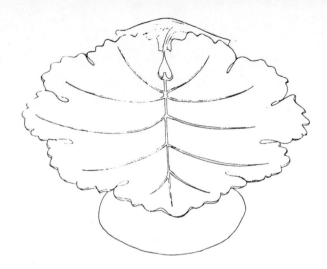

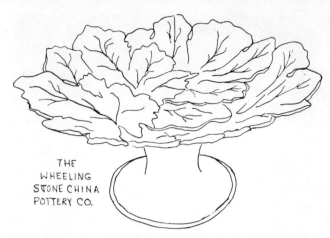

These two low compotes are well potted for American pieces. The Brunt dish is also found without the foot.

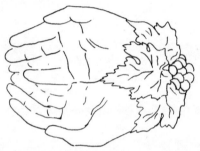

This dish was pictured in Barret's book on Bennington wares, "Extremely rare Graniteware hand dish, 7″ long, 5″ wide." (Has been copied in white milk glass.) Collection of Margie Watson.

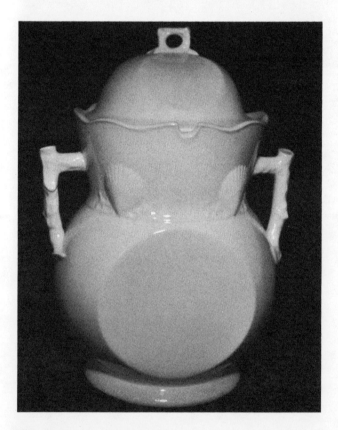

This appears to be an American-made waste jar from a toilet set. Photograph: Black.

IRONSTONE CHINA
J.M. & Co.

American-made, large rectangular soup tureen, tray, and ladle were potted by the Glasgow Pottery Co. of Trenton, New Jersey, founded in 1863. J. M. & Co. referred to John Moses & Co. The jardiniere was unmarked, as are many of the American made pieces.

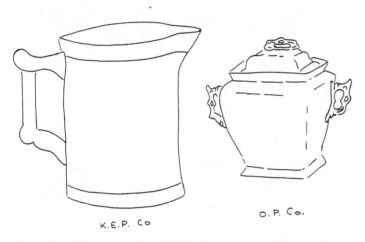

K.E.P. Co

O. P. Co.

Left: Hotel pitcher, marked K. E. P. Co., was a utilitarian piece made by most American white ironstone potters. Right: Square sugar bowl potted by the Onondaga Pottery Co.

Unmarked cup forms were shaped into an invalid feeder (top) and a hand spittoon (below). Grotesque face (or similar masks) circled the hole used to clean a plain, large spittoon made in the States.

19 Gallery of Unusual Pieces

This chapter gives you a special chance to view dishes that you seldom see.

Fruit Garden. Potted by J. F. Barrow & Co. These plates were completely covered by fruit, foliage, and blooms. Even the background was stippled.

Relish dish by Barrow & Co. Footed compote has been seen in this pattern.

Lily Pad. J. W. Pankhurst. This unusual, profusely decorated pattern was used on plates, a high pedestalled compote, and a three-legged cookie plate.

Lily Pad design, three-legged cookie plate by J. W. Pankhurst. This design was also potted in a taller pedestalled compote. Photograph: Blair.

Flower Blanket. This floral composition is done in gleaming white. These plates are probably part of a tea set.

Shallow finger dips, a Victorian novelty, potted by John Edwards after 1891. Owned by Mr. and Mrs. John Black. Photograph: Black.

Long, slender platters for serving baked fish shown with bone dishes by J. & G. Meakin. Collection of Mr. and Mrs. John Black. Photograph: Black.

Hard-to-find, six-quart punchbowl was potted by Francis Morley between 1845 and 1858. Collectors are Mr. and Mrs. John Black. Photograph: Black.

Nautilus shell spoon warmer, a Victorian solution to frigid morning air and quick-cooling porridge. Most warmers were silver plated, made around the turn of the century. According to Dorothy Rainwater in a 1977 article, "Some few were made of sterling silver, some of Britannia ware, and occasional ones of porcelain, the latter so highly prized that former owners had them mended in case of breakage." The nautilus shell was the most popular shape. Nautical designs, including buoys, seaweed, coral, tritons, and bi-valve shells such as oyster or the scallop shape used above, were employed. This early ironstone warmer, circa 1880, was acquired by Mr. and Mrs. John Black. Photograph: Black.

Compote with pierced edges by James Edwards, 9½" in diameter, and 8" high. Collection of Museum of Texas Hand Made Furniture. Photograph: F. Bridges.

This unusual plate is kept warm by hot water poured through the side spout. The word "ironstone" can be read in the impressed mark, but the other words are indecipherable. Probably of English origin. Photograph: Black.

Low basketweave cake plate or doughnut stand stamped Cork, Edge & Malkin. Museum of Texas Hand Made Furniture, New Braunfels, Texas. Photograph: F. Bridges.

Reticulated fruit bowl in **Pierced Scroll** *marked John & Samuel Alcock, Jr., who potted from 1848 to 1850. Photograph: Blair.*

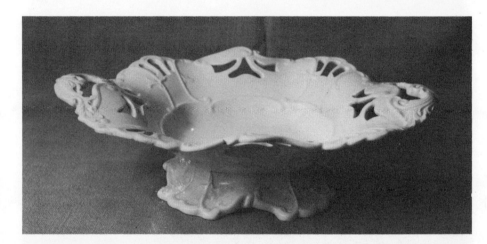

Lower fruit server with different base in **Pierced Scroll,** *marked Alcock, Imperial Stone China. This pattern has been seen on a flat cake plate. Photograph: Blair.*

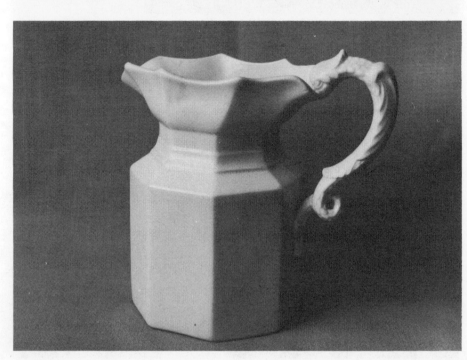

The shape of this **Fenton** *jug by J. Wedgwood was used by the Mason potters. Note the popular snake handle. Collection of Howard and Dorothy Noble. Photograph: Blair.*

English cake plate by T. & R. Boote. It looks like **Chinese Shape,** *but is not marked. Collection of Dick and Adele Armbruster. Photograph: Blair.*

Unique James Edwards china basket decorated with **Open Roses.** *Collection of Colleen James. Photograph: Blair.*

Deep, footed fruit bowl with large individual matching bowls in **One Big and Two Little Ribs** *pattern by Elsmore & Forster in the last years of their potting venture (1851–1871). Thomas Elsmore, their successor, also made this shape. Photograph: Blair.*

175

Pierced fruit holder by T. J. & J. Mayer, 8½" tall. Photograph: Blair.

Tiny compote in **One Big and Two Little Ribs** by Elsmore & Forster in front of **Gothic** dinner plate by J. Alcock. Photograph: Groff.

Little footed server by James Edwards. Photograph: Blair.

Unmarked white ironstone openwork fruit basket. Discovered by Armbrusters, Michigan. Photograph: Armbruster.

Fig dishes potted by J. Wedgwood or Davenport. From an exhibit at the Fort Plain Museum, Fort Plain, New York. Photograph: Blair.

20 One Hundred Years of Ironstone

Nothing follows in history more surely after love of colour than colour weariness and a tendency to renunciation of colour.

—Hannover

An English ceramics historian writes that the "main story of the nineteenth century is bone china." Others have called the 1850s to 1900 period "the Golden Age of Porcelain." None of the historians mentioned ironstone in their accounts. Nevertheless, ironstone wares were manufactured and shipped, ton after ton, to Canada and the United States all through the 1800s.

L. Jewitt and G. Godden are two researchers who have preserved the stories of the Staffordshire potters and their humble stone china production.

Turner's patent china was made public in 1800. Soon similar bodies were discovered by Spode, Davenport, and Hicks & Meigh. However, it was the timely patent in 1813 by Charles James Mason that really launched the age of ironstone.

At first, most of the colorful decorations imitated the Chinese; some being "cribbed" or adapted from the oriental originals that had been imported through the close of the eighteenth century. In England, there was a large middle-class market for this hardy, gaily colored tableware. Some of the patterns used by these potters and their contemporaries were marked *Japan Pattern* or something similar. Many boasted an underglaze cobalt blue design, other colors were applied by hand over the glaze, with an extra trip to the kiln. Students of these early ironstone offerings should study *Godden's Guide to Mason's China and the Ironstone Wares*.

When ceramics trade quickened again shortly after the War of 1812, firms in Staffordshire began to offer flow-blue scenes named after American events or locations (although sometimes there was little resemblance to the actual place).

Mulberry one-color transfer wares. **Pelew** *ironstone by E. Challinor. Photograph: Blair.*

High-relief white stoneware jugs were molded from 1835 to 1870. Rich, flamboyant embossments covered the whole body, and the handles were shaped into branches, serpents, or animals. Most were made of the new Parian wares, but some were made of ironstone. These were made by Wm. Ridgway, T. & R. Boote, Charles Meigh, T. J. & J. Mayer, Holland & Green, J. & M. P. Bell, Cork & Edge, Minton and Copeland, and by the Bennington, Vermont, potters in the 1850s. They rarely are found in America today.

From approximately 1830 to 1860, one-color transfer wares were sold. The mulberry and light blue proved most popular, but sets were also colored in purple, red, green, sepia, or black. These wares overlapped with the all-white ironstone. Occasionally, you may see the same shape both in white and colored with a one-color transfer decoration.

In the mid-1800s, the French potters offered a hard, durable gray white porcelain. Afraid of losing their vast colonial market, the Staffordshire firms made a great effort to produce a more competitive all-white ironstone. Perhaps James Edwards, with his variety of shapes, and Thomas and Richard Boote, with their well-designed, gleaming glazed patterns, led that battle. The beautiful pieces that tempt us today are taken from countless sets potted during the productive white ironstone years, 1840 to 1870. Here were wares that could stand the rigors of the westward movement: swaying covered wagons, river rafts, mule trains, and early railroad baggage cars.

By 1855, the *Sydenham Shape* and its relatives had won the hearts of American housewives, and white ironstone became "naturalized." Then English potters, clever men that they were, remembered how the Americans had clamored for the ceramic blue-and-white American scenes produced a few decades earlier. They began to design ironstone shapes whose names connotated Americanism: *Columbia, President, Union, LaFayette,* and *Atlantic.* Some cities were honored by marks reading *New York Shape, Paris Shape, St. Louis Shape,* or *Montpelier Shape.* Two states were highlighted in the impressed marks of *Virginia Shape* and *Kansas Shape.* Often panels, ribs, and scallops were included in the most popular lines during these years.

In the late 1850s and throughout the 1860s, potters used realistic motifs from forest leaves, orchard fruits, nuts, grains, and garden blooms—a sort of celebration of a succulent earth.

Roman or Greek influences were found in wreaths, well-known key designs, or fleur-de-lis lines in the late 1860s. Half a dozen patterns included narrow ribbing covering much of the body and were bordered by berries, chains, or buds. Because the registry dates were omitted in the markings, we are unable to pinpoint the age of these ribbed decorations.

Then came the Civil War and the sad years of austerity that follow an internal conflict. Money was short. Ironstone was no longer a novelty, but the English wares were

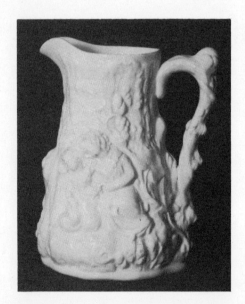

High relief stoneware jug with a **Babes in the Woods** scene by Cork & Edge. Collection of Ray & Priscilla Casavant. Photograph: Groff.

*Beautiful **Strawberry** pattern in gaudy ironstone by Elsmore & Forster. "Skip" Barshied from New York State recalls that this was "My great-grandmother's wedding china in the early 1850s." Photograph: Blair.*

Fifty years of white ironstone shapes. Potted in the early 1840s, the first shapes were Gothic, as shown in the upper left-hand corner. The bottom examples reveal the influences of ribs, scallops, fruits, grains, foliage, and flowers. The dishes in the upper right-hand corner were potted in the clean, simple lines of the 1880s. Photograph: Blair, Fort Plain Museum, Fort Plain, New York.

still inexpensive. Gradually, those who could afford better, more beautiful dishes began to refer derogatively to the plain ware as "thrasher's china." It was true that the people from rural areas continued to serve their food on this hardy earthenware for more decades.

As soon as the fate of the Union was settled, stirrings of a strong national feeling were felt all over America. Despite high tariffs, England still wooed the United States china market. A period of plain white ironstone designs was introduced. The graceful round pear-shaped bodies were generally undecorated; rectangular shapes became more popular. These changes were adopted during the 1870s and 1880s, as the American pottery businesses were becoming more stable.

At the close of the century, a few more detailed designs on lighter weight white ironstone were introduced by the Staffordshire potters. Much hotel ware was made to satisfy commercial needs, but in general, the age of white ironstone popularity had passed.

During the 1850s, companies such as Elsmore & Forster and Edw. Walley embellished their ironstone shapes with bright colors. Today we call this *Gaudy Ironstone*. The best-known patterns are *Strawberry, Blackberry, Seeing Eye, Grape, Sunflower, Urn,* and some *Imari* types. These treasures are now very expensive.

Marbleized transfers over whole bodies, usually the *Gothic Shape,* were employed by Anthony Shaw, Alcock, J. Wedgwood, Hulme & Booth, Venable & Baines, and others.

Elsmore & Forster used two deep-purple transfer patterns over their *Arched Forget-Me-Not* and *Gothic* shapes. Wishful devotees search for these regularly. *Arched Forget-Me-Not* blanks were used under the transfers.

Gleaming gray marbleized toilet set over an impressed forget-me-not embellishment. Unmarked, but may have been an Alcock or Meier work. Photograph: Blair.

*Deep-purple transfer dishes in **Trumpet Flowers** by Elsmore & Forster, potted in the 1850s. Photograph: Groff.*

In the 1860s, Anthony Shaw, J. Clementson, and Elsmore & Forster began to experiment with copper lustre bands, with and without motifs. The now-famous *Copper Tea Leaf* (discussed in detail in Chapter Seventeen) was applied by Anthony Shaw, became popular, and was copied by many English and American firms during the last quarter of the nineteenth century.

By the end of the decade, many American families hungrily accepted the brown-and-white or brown-and-ivory sets of cheap, lighter-weight ironstone to use as everyday dishes.

About this time, a "Japonaiserie" cult affected decorations on silver, glass, and china. Examinations of the brown-and-white patterns made from 1877 to 1883 show consistent repetition of bamboo stalks, cherry branches, oriental sailboats, exotic birds, fans, geometric bands, and sometimes a section resembling a crazy quilt. Modern collectors laughingly refer to these dishes as "Japanese Patchwork." Occasionally, a pattern was executed in a medium blue or gray, but brown and white were the colors of that day. Almost every design also included a small round or square picture of a scene or an animal.

For the following six or seven years, evenly balanced border designs were employed. They were in the same browns and white, with leaves or flowers. By the 1890s, the brown styles changed to large naturalistic branches on one border of a plate, echoed by a smaller branch opposite.

Closely related in color and design to **Trumpet Flowers** *is* **Grandmother's Flowers** *by Elsmore & Forster, also potted in the 1850s. Photograph: Groff.*

A pair of brown-and-white "Japanese Patchwork" patterns, registered 1881. Fun collectibles. Photograph: Blair.

A close study of the brown-and-white transfers actually can date the pieces within a year or so, because Staffordshire potters followed popular styles so closely during these years. Most of the colored ironstone dishes from these decades are clearly marked with names and dates. As other collectibles grow scarce, I predict this field will become of interest to ironstone hoarders.

Used on white ironstone, the motifs of grains, fruits, berries, meadow flowers, and lush vines may have been designed to please the cottage dwellers or decorate the tables of farm families. Three-dimensional finials of ripe fruits, nuts, ears of corn, bursting seed pods, and gourds symbolized fertile soil and productive gardens and fields.

Today, some of this aura of plenteous harvest is a connotation of the sturdy ironstone. We envision mounds of fluffy potatoes heaped in large vegetable dishes, savory stews, arranged on great white platters, roomy two-quart milk pitchers that really pour, homemade relishes and jams filling boat or leaf-shaped servers, and of course, homemade vegetable soup or corn chowder to be ladled out of great tureens. We daydream of crisp homegrown farm products, the aroma of fresh baked bread, plates of sliced tomatoes, and waving fields of grain, and think that these solid, durable dishes can somehow bring back those departed days. Personally, I think we only want the memories—not the drafty houses, hours of backbreaking labor, or hours of preparation for large family meals. But a slice of homemade bread would taste good, wouldn't it?

The popularity of country life has swung full circle in the last hundred years. Farmers used to look forward to the day when they could leave the homestead and the hard work and move to town. Today, the city dwellers long to vacation or retire in the good country air. The epithet "thrasher's china" has been exchanged for the charm of those "beautiful blue-white dishes" that Great Grandma used.

Still Looking

We use our eyes and minds to look again and again. Long after I thought all of the information for this book was organized and recorded, collectors continued to send a drawing or a snapshot or a copy of a potter's mark.

Bill Neuhauser from New Jersey recently sent three pictures from his lengthy white ironstone pitcher parade. One shows a J. F. milk jug with lines so deeply impressed that we call it the *Grand Loop*.

I wonder if it could be related to an unmarked cover that I've been keeping for years.

Grand Loop milk jug by J. F. with deeply impressed lines. Courtesy Bill Neuhauser.

Unmarked cover from author's collection.

His second photograph was one of a ewer clearly marked *Garibaldi Shape* registered by T. & R. Boote on December 23, 1860. The leaf that decorates the 1861 Boote pattern (page 89), *Winding Vine*, looks very similar.

Garibaldi Shape ewer registered December 23, 1860, by T. & R. Boote. Courtesy Bill Neuhauser.

Bill's third photograph was of an American-made syrup pitcher with a pewter lid, manufactured by Knowles, Taylor & Knowles in 1880. Most of our native potters kept their lines simple and undecorated by impressed designs.

American-made syrup pitcher, pewter lid, by Knowles, Taylor & Knowles, 1880. Courtesy Bill Neuhauser.

In contrast, the drawing is of a recently found unnamed pattern on a syrup pitcher with pewter lid that was made by the English firm, Livesley & Powell, between 1851 and 1866.

LIVESLEY & POWELL
1851-1866
7" tall, 2½" wide

One of the earliest white ironstone shapes (we nicknamed it *Primary*) was used in the late 1830s and early 1840s. This is pictured in the form of a sugar bowl made by John Ridgway & Co. The piece is marked by a wreath cartouche encircling the words "Porcelaine a la Francais," in answer to powerful French competition for colonial trade during the first half of the nineteenth century.

*Sugar bowl in early ironstone shape (nicknamed **Primary**) by John Ridgway & Co., circa 1830.*

There will always remain mysteries unsolved. Those divided deep bowls with holes that suggest two hinged pewter covers? Could they have been pretzel bowls? Did J. Goodwin refer to John Goodwin (of Seacombe Pottery) or to lesser-known Joseph Goodwin? And the oft-asked question: Does J. F. really refer to Jacob Furnival? I think so, basing my premise on the fact that a few patterns have been found marked J. F. that match similar dishes marked Furnival. Keep watch.

Certainly our eyes will continue to help us learn even more than can be found in this *Second Look at White Ironstone.*

Bibliography

Barber, Edwin Atlee. *Marks of American Potters*. Reprint. Southampton, New York: Cracker Barrel Press, 1968.

Barber, Edwin Atlee. *Pottery and Porcelain of the United States*. New York: G.P. Putnam's Sons, 1893.

Barret, Richard Carter. *Bennington Pottery and Porcelain*. New York: Crown Publishers, Inc. 1958.

Burton, William, F. CS. *A History of English Earthenware and Stoneware*. London: Cassell & Co. Ltd., 1904.

Chaffers, William. *Marks and Monograms on Pottery and Porcelain*. London: Bickers & Son, 1876.

Church, Arthur H. *English Earthenware Made During the 17th and 18th Century*. Revised Edition. London: Wyman and Sons, 1904.

Cole, Ann Kilborn. *How to Collect the New Antiques*. New York: David McKay Co., Inc., 1966.

Collard, Elizabeth. *Nineteenth Century Pottery and Porcelain in Canada*. Montreal: McGill University Press, 1967.

Drepperd, Carl. *The Primer of American Antiques*. Garden City, New York: Doubleday & Co., Inc. 1944.

Earle, Alice Morse. *China Collecting in America*. New York: Empire State Book Co., 1924.

Eberlein and Ramsdell. *The Practical Book of Chinaware*. Philadelphia and New York: J. B. Lippincott Co., 1925.

Godden, Geoffrey. *Antique Glass and China*. New York: Castle Books, 1966.

Godden, Geoffrey A. F. R. S. A. *Encyclopaedia of British Pottery and Porcelain Marks*. New York: Crown Publishers, Inc. 1964.

———. *Godden's Guide to Mason's China and the Ironstone Wares*. Church Street, Woodbridge, Suffolk, England: Baron Publishing, 1980.

Graham II, John Meredith and Wedgwood, Hensleigh Cecil. *Wedgwood*. New York: The Tudor Publishing Co., 1948.

Hayden, Arthur. *Chats on English China*. London: T. Fisher Unwin Ltd., 1904.

Heaivilin, Annise Doring. *Grandma's Tea Leaf Ironstone*. Des Moines: Wallace-Homestead Book Co., 1981.

Hudgeons, Thomas E., III. *Price Guide to Pottery and Porcelain*, 3rd ed. Orlando, Florida: House of Collectibles.

Hughes, Bernard and Therle. *Encyclopedia of English Ceramics*. London: Lutterworth Press, 1956.

Kamm, Minnie Watson. *Old China*. Grosse Pointe, Mich.: Kamm Publications, 1951.

Ketchum, Wm. Jr. *The Pottery and Porcelain Collector's Handbook*. New York: Funk & Wagnall's, 1971.

Klamkin, Marian. *American Patriotic and Political China*. New York: Charles Scribners & Sons, 1973.

Lewis, Griselda. *A Collector's History of English Pottery*. New York: The Viking Press, 1969.

Mankowitz, Wolf and Haggar, Reginald. *Concise Encyclopedia of English Pottery and Porcelain*. New York: Hawthorn Books, Inc. 1957.

McClinton, Katherine Morrison. *A Handbook of Popular Antiques*. Reprint. New York: Random House, 1965. Distr. by Crown Pub., Inc.

———. *Antiques, Past and Present*. New York: Clarkson N. Pottery, Inc. 1971.

Moore, N. Hudson. *The Old China Book*. New York: Tudor Publishing Co., 1903.

Nelson, Glenn. *Ceramics*. New York: Holt, Rinehart, and Winston, Inc., 1971.

Ramsay, John. *American Potters and Potteries.* Clinton, Massachusetts: Hale, Cushman & Flint, 1939.

Raycraft, Donald R. *Early American Folk & Country Antiques.* Vermont, Japan: Charles E. Tuttle Co., Inc. 1971.

Reynolds, Ernest. *Collecting Victorian Porcelain.* New York: Frederick A. Praeger, 1966.

Sandon, Henry. *British Pottery and Porcelain for Pleasure and Investment.* New York: Arco Publishing Co., Inc. 1969.

Spargo, John. *Early American Pottery and China.* Reprint. New York: Garden City Pub. Co., Inc. 1948.

Thorn, C. Jordan. *Handbook of Old Pottery and Porcelain Marks.* New York: Tudor Publishing Co., 1947.

Watkins, Lura Woodside. *New England Potters and Their Wares.* Boston: Archon Books, 1968 reprint.

Wetherbee, Jean. *A Look at White Ironstone.* Des Moines: Wallace-Homestead Book Co., 1980.

Magazines

"American Ceramic and the Philadelphia Exhibition." *Antiques,* July 1976, pp. 146-158.

Collard, Elizabeth. "The St. Johns Stone Chinaware Company." *Antiques,* October 1976, pp. 800-805.

Meissen-Helter, Pauline. "What Is Ironstone?" Unpublished.

Rainwater, Dorothy T. "Spoon Warmers," *Spinning Wheel,* October 1977, p. 35.

Index

About the Author

Jean Wetherbee was born in Canajoharie (Indians called it, "the pot that washes itself") in the scenic Mohawk Valley of New York. Later, she and her husband Bernard reared four children on the six-generation family farm in that historic area. They declared, "A farm is the best place on earth to raise a family." Her love of the earth, joy in growing things, and interests in the past are reflected in her writings.

A former teacher and reading specialist, her interest in white ironstone evolved from her own collecting and curiosity about the origin of this hardy ware. Facts gathered in research were compiled in *A Handbook on White Ironstone* (1974) and *A Look at White Ironstone* (1980). This second look is a continuation of that investigation.

Wetherbee is involved with a small white ironstone location service and enjoys painting with a country touch. She does volunteer work for ADRDA, an association dedicated to bringing Alzheimer's Disease out of the darkness. She makes her home in the Boston suburb of Andover, Massachusetts.